WHAT'S YOUR WHEELCHAIR?

WHAT'S YOUR WHEELCHAIR?

Amy Alexander

Contributing Editor – Edison Guzman

What's Your Wheelchair, Inc.
Published 2014

First Printing: 2014

ISBN: 978-0-9916079-0-7

What's Your Wheelchair, Inc.
P.O. Box 566
Pine Bush, NY 12566

www.WhatsYourWheelchair.com

Ordering Information:

Special discounts are available on quantity purchases by corporations, associations, educators, and others. For details, contact the publisher at the above listed address.

U.S. trade bookstores and wholesalers:
Please contact What's Your Wheelchair, Inc.
Tel: (845) 744 – 6550; or email bookorders@whatsyourwheelchair.com.

*I'd like to dedicate this book to all of the individuals
who are works in progress, on the path to
creating the life of their dreams.*

*And when you dream...
Remember to dream big!
Please know I am right there with you
and your biggest fan.*

Table of Contents

INTRODUCTION

As individuals, we are all works in progress. Each of us experience challenges in life we strive to overcome. Some of these challenges are temporary, others are permanent.

Twenty years ago, I was in a car accident. I sustained a spinal cord injury, paralyzing me for the rest of my life. I was twenty-one years old.

I would be lying if I said being paralyzed doesn't come with its challenges. The key to overcoming them is the ability to recognize them.

We all experience wheelchairs in life. Some are hard to see. Others are more obvious and in-your-face.

What inspired me to write "What's Your Wheelchair" is regardless of how large or small, how obvious or obscure, life's wheelchairs do not need to be a barrier from achieving our dreams and being happy.

Everyone has the ability to overcome the obstacles blocking our goals. This has nothing to do with the size of the obstacle or the size of the goal. It has to do with our *personal power.*

Each of us possess our own unique personal power. It's not something we work to achieve. It's innate within all of us.

The only thing we need to do is *recognize* it and then *apply* it. It's one of the few things in life that is truly priceless and actually free. And the more you use it, the more powerful it becomes.

Just as important in recognizing our personal power is recognizing our wheelchairs. If we can't identify our challenges, it's impossible to avoid them. And avoiding them is sidestepping the land mine that will blowup your dreams.

I'll share what used to be one of my greatest challenges, and blew up my dreams many times. My titanium wheelchair is permanent, and there is nothing I can do about it. The choices I make regarding how I live my life in it, however, are entirely mine.

The key to living a healthy life when you have a spinal cord injury is *prevention*. Prevention is everything. If you do not prevent second-ary issues that can manifest, those issues will take everything from you... your goals, your dreams, your hard work thusfar...even your life.

Time and time again, my hard work at creating the life I wished was snuffed out in an instant by a life threatening secondary health issue I could have prevented. I was forced to start from ground zero more times then I can count.

My "wheelchair" was I had my priorities entirely out of order. I would work myself to the bone, ignore the very clear signs my body was giving me until I was so sick, my life was at risk.

Secondary health issues don't just happen overnight. Your body gives subtle but very clear signs of, "Hello! I need a little attention!" I would ignore the signs because I couldn't admit my body was no longer capable of keeping up with my brain.

After dozens of preventable sufferings, surgeries and hospital stays, common sense kicked it. (I'm a little stubborn.) The great thing about secondary issues is if you give them attention as soon as they present themselves, they are no big deal.

At worst, you alter your schedule for a day or two, adding a bit of rest and subtracting a bit of work. That's it.

As I continue to keep my priorities straight, my life has changed for the better in a so many significant ways. I hadn't realized how true it is our health is the foundation for all of the other components in our life.

My health, my work, and even my relationships have blossomed by using my personal power to make changes where changes were necessary. I no longer take ten steps forward and then twenty back.

We are all works in progress. My hope is by sharing some of my life's experiences with you, you will come to believe...Believe regardless of the number, size and shape of your wheelchairs, the power is within you, *right this very moment*, to *not* allow them to hold you back from achieving your greatest dreams.

Chapter 1:
A DOSE OF ENTHUSIASM

Those Who Go Above and Beyond

Good home healthcare aides are a rarity. Phenomenal ones are on the extinction list. I have had the experience of working with both. This article is dedicated to a group of girls who got me through the hardest time in my life. The death of my father.

My dad and I were very close. He was one of my best friends, loved his family unconditionally and drove us absolutely crazy. Particularly near the end of his life.

Dad lived with colon cancer for seven years. I say lived because it's exactly what he did. He had surgeries, radiation and chemotherapy. He had hospital stays and life-threatening infections. Somewhere in there, he also had a heart attack.

At the same time he had cancer, he had two grandchildren he adored. He went to swim meets, baseball games, softball games, school concerts and never missed a birthday party. He *lived* with cancer.

As it does with many people living with cancer, there may come a point when the cancer is getting stronger than the person. It becomes clear you are at a point of no return.

To me, this point came for my father about four months prior to him passing away. I could just feel after every infection, every hospital stay, every exhausting treatment, he got weaker and weaker and didn't recover to be strong enough for the next hurdle.

For the last year of Dad's life, I had the three best aides I ever worked with. Not only were they phenomenal aides with me, they were phenomenal to my father and my family. These are three of the rare people in the world who go above and beyond without being asked. It's just who they are.

My dad was a very big hearted, warm man. He was very easy to like. Even my mom, who is his ex-wife, will say this. Everybody loved Frank.

He also drove me crazier than any human ever has or ever will. There is a picture of him on a mule in the dictionary next to the word "stubborn." This genetic gift was never more flamboyant than when Dad had cancer.

The worse Dad's cancer became, the worse his stubbornness became. Dad needed some home healthcare, and he adamantly refused. He did not expect nor want his children to take care of him, either. He was going to take care of himself.

My aides were so great. I rented an apartment above my father, in his home. During the day, we started hearing a bang or a crash coming from downstairs. I'd call him on the phone to see if he was okay. He was fine… he had dropped something, or something fell off a shelf, blah blah blah.

We started becoming suspicious. If we heard a bang, my aide started running downstairs and would be in my dad's living room in three or four seconds. They started finding him on the floor because he had lost his balance.

Dad was sneaky. He had been falling down for a while. However, he counted on the time it took me to get downstairs via my elevator. In that time, he could get himself off the floor and onto his couch or his recliner.

Dad started falling a lot. He fell on a baseboard heater and had third-degree burns all over his back. He fell in the bathroom, split his head open and needed stitches.

It became a routine. When we heard a bang upstairs, my aide would run downstairs and assess the situation. Then, they would come back upstairs and we would go downstairs together.

During the ride in the elevator, they'd filled me in on Dad's situation. Sometimes I would call 911 while I was still in the elevator, and sometimes I would have a look at him first. There were times he was lucky I was paralyzed because I wanted to strangle him.

We had family interventions with him. We talked with him one on one. We cried, we begged, we pleaded with him to allow us to hire some help. He let us say our piece, let us go on and on and on and at the end, say nothing. Just give us the bland look we had seen all our lives and we knew what it meant.

We had one thing on our side. He loved my three aides. Cameron, Leah and Joanie. He had known them for a while, so they were not strangers invading his home.

The three girls just casually aided Dad during their shifts with whatever he needed. Dad and I started eating dinner together every night instead of our usual twice a week, so he didn't have to cook. They would bring a sandwich downstairs with salad or soup for lunch because I happened to have extra.

When Dad fell, they picked him up. When he needed to go to the hospital, they would get his pill list and his favorite sweater. They did so many things my heart wanted to do but my hands could not.

When Dad was in the hospital, they drove me everyday to visit him. Regardless driving me was part of their job, they wanted to see him as much as I did. And vice versa.

Dad came home from the hospital five days before he passed away. The girls helped me decorate his room, clean the house and plant extra flowers. It was late September and the mums were stunning.

The girls sat with Dad and talked to him, even when he was no longer awake. When he left us, they cooked, they cleaned and at times, held me upright.

When Dad started needing help, my family and I repeatedly told the girls taking care of Dad was not part of their job. It didn't matter; they kept doing what they were doing. We made sure they were compensated for it, but as Joanie said, "This is just a bonus."

They went above and beyond out of love, out of caring. I could not have made it through my dad's illness and leaving us if it not for those three beautiful souls. Thank you, girls. You have my love and gratitude forever.

Check Out This Action – The Action Trackchair

When I was initially injured, I had a very scary experience in my power wheelchair. It malfunctioned and caught on fire. I was physically fine, but emotionally was not. It was years before I could use a power chair again.

When I made the decision to get back in a power chair saddle, I was not prepared for the impact it would have. I had used a manual wheelchair for so long... I was not strong enough to push it, so it offered me zero independence.

Using a power wheelchair changed my life. I was no longer dependent on someone for every little move I wished to make. I experienced a degree of physical independence for the first time since being injured.

It also improved my health significantly. My power wheelchair could assist my body in changing positions. This allowed circulation to the places on a wheelchair user's body receiving the most pressure from constantly sitting.

Fast forward to the year 2014. Now there is an even higher tier of independence offered to wheelchair users. More than independence, it offers *fun*. It's called the Action Trackchair. It's amazing.

Your average power wheelchair is limited to flat surfaces. Mine is said to be perfectly capable in making a smooth transition over a three inch curb. I tried it the first day I got my chair... The transition was so unsteady, I lost my balance and fell over.

The developers of the Action Trackchair designed their product based on what an individual wants to do. They looked way, way beyond wheels and the limits of a flat surfaced world.

They looked at what the world is made up of and how to create something that could navigate through as much of it as possible. The more their product could navigate through, the more the user could experience.

The Action Trackchair allows wheelchair users to enjoy outdoor activities they may have done prior to becoming disabled. The genius of the Trackchair is instead of having wheels, it has tracks, similar to an army tank.

Flat surfaces, move over! This ATW (all-terrain wheelchair) gives the user the ultimate experience in off road wheelchairs. Folks can go places they never thought possible. This allows an individual to enjoy the outdoors and not miss out by being able to go beyond flat borders.

The Action Trackchair will plow you through mountain roads, campgrounds, woods, beaches, hiking trails, streams, snow, mud and beyond!

I have yet to experience the Action Trackchair, but I cannot wait until I do! The thought of being able to go on the beach without having to be carried is a dream for me! Going to where the surf meets the sand on my own is something I have not been able to do in twenty years.

Many times, going on a Sunday drive leads Mike and I to a park where hiking is available. The Action Trackchair would allow me to go through the woodsy terrain without worrying about coming across mud, bumps and small streams.

Living in the Northeast, we also get our share of snowstorms. My wheelchair is useless in the snow. The trackchair would allow me to trample through the snow and enjoy the winter fun.

Not only is there the Action Trackchair... there is also the Action Trackstander. This ATW allows an individual to not only go where they want to go, but they can *stand* along the way. With the Action Trackchair and Action Trackstander, disabled individuals are given the freedom to partake in so many activities their disability took away.

Tim Swenson is the developer of the Action Trackchair and the Action Trackstander. His own son was disabled in a car accident many years ago. Tim and his wife moved forward in helping their son gain back his independence. Through that process came these amazing Trackchairs.

Currently, insurance companies and Medicare do not pay for the Action Trackchairs. They are not yet convinced these chairs meet their bureaucratic functional guidelines. They need a lesson in the *fun* of *fun*ction.

The more awareness the Action Trackchair and the Action Trackstander receive as a product offering functionality to disabled individuals, the greater the chance of private insurance and Medicare paying for them.

How do you create awareness? Write your congressman or local representative and let them know how you feel about Medicare and insurance companies limiting guidelines.

Visit their website at www.actiontrackchair.com. Watch the videos of both the Action Trackchair and the Action Trackstander. Then, imagine yourself in a wheelchair only capable of going on flat surfaces.

Imagine how limited you would be. As you watch the videos and read the testimonials of current Action Trackchair users, imagine how your world would open up if you were the user of one.

Thank you to the Action Trackchair developers and all those who look beyond the limits of a flat surfaced world and instead, look at the real world disabled people live in.

You Can't See Hair Grow

We live in a society where instant gratification takes too long. We do our best to get everything we need, wish or want yesterday. There are circumstances, however, where forces greater than us take over and instant gratification is replaced with baby steps. Grasshopper baby steps.

Sustaining a spinal cord injury was one of those circumstances. Prior to being injured, I lived life going in ten different directions at once. Get a mental picture of how the Tazmanian Devil moves around and you have an accurate depiction of me.

Well, the brakes went on when I was injured. My body stopped moving, and there wasn't anything I could do about it. My doctors explained to me the medical community did not know how to fix a spinal cord injury, plain and simple. But they did say I would slowly get better and heal.

The not knowing how to fix a spinal cord injury I understood right away. I had an injury, causing permanent paralysis, and currently there was no known cure. What's not to understand? Doctors are human, not magicians.

It was the "slowly get better and heal" aspect I wrestled with. If you couldn't fix me, what was there to possibly heal? I couldn't move anything. I couldn't feel anything. What was going to change?

I didn't understand at the time the degree of shock my body received. Our spinal cord controls so much more than just our movement and sensation. It controls our breathing, regulates our temperature and aides in digestion. Simply put, getting a spinal cord injury initially kicks your body's ass.

I was as weak as a newborn kitten. My body needed time to rest and get strong again. Sustaining a spinal cord injury is being reborn with a body that works very differently than your old one. You need time to learn how your new body works. This process doesn't happen in leaps and bounds. It happens in baby steps.

To look for improvement is torture. To "see" progress in the acute phase of a spinal cord injury, you would need to plant a camera in your hospital room and let it record for about month. Then, you would need to fast forward so the entire month viewed in about fifteen minutes.

One day I was having a particularly challenging time all around; physically, mentally and emotionally. The name of the nurse I had was Ann. Twenty years later, this memory is as clear to me as today.

Ann could tell I was struggling to keep myself together. She pulled a chair up to my bedside and asked me if I wanted to talk. She had perfect timing.

I told her I understood my spinal cord could not be fixed. But I told her I was really struggling with believing how I was going to heal enough and get strong enough and progress enough to get out of the hospital and have some sort of life.

When I shared my fears with my doctors, (who were family by this point), they assured me things would get better. It was just an extremely slow process, and unfortunately, I would just have to do the time.

I told Ann I could deal with that if I could only *believe* it. I had been in the hospital for over a month at this point and I still felt as weak as a kitten. And I was trying my hardest to just let time take over and work its magic, but I was failing.

Ann listened without interruption. When I had gotten everything off my chest, she was thoughtful for a moment. Then she said, "Well, you can't see hair grow, but we all know it does."

Some how those words shifted my perception effortlessly. I worked hard, and time went by. I spent three months in acute care, three months at a rehabilitation center, then home.

I got stronger, I healed and I have a life. A *beautiful* life. I never saw Ann again after I left the hospital. That was twenty years ago. I wish I knew her last name to attempt to find her. I would be so happy to tell her she saved my life. She shined the first light for me in a very, very dark place.

No Excuse Resolutions

At the start of each New Year, most of us have a few resolutions in mind. With good intentions, we think of ways we can improve ourselves and our world around us. Unfortunately, the majority of us do not put these "resolutionary" ideas into action. Why is that?

Some of the more popular resolutions I repeatedly hear are losing weight, exercise more, get organized, spend more time with the kids, keep better in touch with friends, get out of debt, quit smoking or drinking or simply to enjoy life more. All fantastic ideas, no doubt.

I have made and not kept as many resolutions as the next person. A few years ago, however, I was actually able to follow through with one. It changed my life.

My resolution was to figure out why most of us do not keep New Year's resolutions! Every resolution I have ever heard has been a good idea. Then why are they rarely even started?

Resolutions usually end up being big goals. Lose weight, get out of debt, write your first novel, join the Peace Corps, etc., etc. Goals of that size need a bit of thought to achieve. Bottom line, we need to develop plans to achieve the big goals that are made of baby goals.

Many of us unconsciously set ourselves up for failure by choosing huge resolutions with absolutely no idea how to bring them into fruition. We become overwhelmed and intimidated by the simple thought of our resolution and nothing gets accomplished. We end up feeling worse about ourselves than before we made our resolutions.

To accomplish any goal I set, I need two things; a plan and a touchstone. My dad used to remind me when we were playing chess, a bad plan is better than no plan. Meaning, have a plan in place to reach your final goal.

First, define exactly what your final goal is. Then, with each move you make, check yourself to ensure it's in the direction of your goal. If you find one of your steps is not in alignment, simply realign it.

Make deadlines for yourself. *Realistic* deadlines. Reward yourself for meeting each one. Just as important, if you find yourself experiencing a challenging day, and you've gone off in the wrong direction, don't throw in the towel. Simply think about what you need to change to get back on your goal path, and continue on from there.

We all fall off the wagon at times. The important thing is not to give up. I've had countless instances of taking ten steps forward and then two steps back. I try my best to look at it as eight steps forward, with a small learning curve thrown in.

Next, you need a touchstone. Someone you can connect with to help you define your big goal, assist with your initial baby step plan and touch base with along the way so you don't feel alone in your efforts.

It's human to need encouragement. I consider myself a pretty self-motivated person. It would be difficult, however, to continually move forward without someone I can converse with regarding ideas, setbacks and possible changes I may need to make.

This individual can be anybody, but they should possess some knowledge or desire for what you are doing. With today's technology, you can find this individual over the computer via forums, message boards and chat rooms without ever having to leave the house.

I wrote my first memoir about five years ago. My touchstone was a young woman I had never met, but was introduced via email through a mutual friend. She was a writer and it was fantastic to have her read my writing and offer her opinion as a fellow writer. Her insight, guidance, brainstorming and cheerleading were priceless. I don't think I could have finished my book without her.

So make your resolutions. Start with one at a time. And then revel in kicking each one's ass. Define your ultimate goal, put together a baby step plan on how to achieve it, find a touchstone and get to work. No excuses.

Precious Disabled Pets

I was recently looking on the web for organizations accepting wheelchairs for donations. Along the way, I stumbled across organizations donating wheelchairs to *pets*. Instantly, an image of Snoopy Red Baron sitting in a wheelchair popped into my mind.

I had to check this out. What I found was an enormous array of support, resources and disabled pet products for individuals who had or were thinking about adopting a pet with a disability or special need.

What inspired me about the organizations were the amount of information existing for every aspect of a disabled pet's needs. There were dozens of categories with different disabilities and chronic conditions pet owners may encounter during the life of their pet.

The organizations had products and services available I would never even think of. There were custom – made wheelchairs, harnesses, boots, holistic healthcare information, the best way to find the right vet and nutrition facts.

There was even a pet hospice section, offering guidance to pet owners dealing with fatal conditions and educating them on what their options were, how much these options cost and which pet insurances cover them.

There was a classified section where people could offer products and services for free and advertise used products for sale. Folks who were looking solely for donated items could also advertise what they needed for their pet.

If you are like us, your pets are part of your family. We have a beautiful sixteen year old, long haired calico cat named Missy. She has the look and stride of Queen of Sheeba and a personality to match.

She is so pretty you can't help but hope she'll like you. If she decides you're one of the chosen few, she will reward you with an effortless jump onto your lap. When she walks across the room, you can cut her arrogance with a knife, and we love her for it.

As pretty as she is, you may expect her to be a prissy, indoor only cat. Not so. Missy is a savage hunter, bringing rabbits, chipmunks, birds and mice to our door. She has burrs matted in her long hair, as proof of the lengths she'll go to in order to capture her prey.

Missy has plenty of fresh food and water at her feet anytime she wishes. Everyone who walks through our door takes one look at her and gives her treats. I've come to believe the reason Missy hunts and is sure to show us her prize is to let me know she is 100% self sufficient.

She *chooses* to stay with her mere humans, but in no way *needs* us. I can't blame her, really...proclaiming independence is important in today's world, especially if you're female.

We have two more pets; a horse and a pony. Our horse's name is Nutmeg, and she was originally my father's. When my father passed away, Nutmeg was supposed to go to our niece. Somehow, she ended up staying with us. No complaints.

Our pony, who is older then Moses, is our third pet. Her name is Maggie. We acquired her from a place who was severely neglecting her. She lived in a wet field with cows and had absolutely no shelter.

She was also fed what the cows were fed, and as a result of the neglect and the severely incorrect diet, Maggie acquired a chronic, degenerative and ultimately fatal hoof disease.

Our Nutmeg needed a companion and Maggie was perfect. We asked Maggie's owner if we could take Maggie off their hands and they gladly said yes. We thanked them for doing us a huge favor by giving us a companion for our horse.

Our little disabled pony is the toughest, sweetest animal I've ever met, and I grew up on a horse farm. She does require special new shoes once a month and daily pain medicine. That makes no difference to us. She will be part of our family for the rest of her life.

Moving Forward In The Wrong Direction

Sitting in traffic is maddening. You usually don't know what the cause of the traffic is or have any idea how long you're going to be stuck in it. An accident could be holding things up, a detour, road-work, lane closure, a bottleneck due to rush hour or a holiday, or it could simply be rubbernecking. You are left to guess. You are also left to wonder how long it is going to last. Wondering is the worst.

The way I see it, you have two choices. Either sit in traffic and wait it out, or take the next available exit and find a different way to your destination. You'd need a crystal ball to tell you which choice would be faster. Even with the modern technology of GPS for finding a different route, there are no guarantees the new route will be shorter due to the same traffic possibilities you were experiencing on the old route.

While it may feel as if you are getting closer to your destination because your car is moving instead of sitting in traffic, be careful. You could be moving forward in the wrong direction and end up further away from your destination than if you would have waited out the traffic. Or you might get frustrated because you have no idea of where are you are headed and just give up, turn around and go home.

I'm starting a new business and am in the process of building its foundation. I have my goals set out clearly in front of me, broken down from the end-all be-all goal, with a step-by-step plan of smaller goals or steps. As I move forward in my process, sometimes I will get an idea I want to ad as another step in the journey of reaching my current goal.

An individual that is helping me with marketing has taught me to stop and take a good look at my step to make sure it's in the direction of my goal. Maybe it's a good idea, many ideas are. But if it is veering me off course in another direction, than that's where I'm going to go… And who knows how long I will be going in the wrong direction before I realize it?

I have had many goals and ideas that never came into fruition, even though I worked very, very hard at them. Looking back, I realize the reason each time was basically the same… I veered myself off course by incorporating an idea (step) into my plan that was in a different direction than my goal. The ideas all seem like good ones, and maybe they were. But they had to be in line with other good ideas that were in the direction of the same goal. If you're working very hard and you aren't getting closer to your goal, you're going to give up and stop, and start something new.

Time will tell if I've learned this lesson enough to make the business I am working on a success. We will see. But I promise, you'll be one of the first to know.

If You Ordered Self-Help, Make Sure That's What You Get

Since my injury, I've attended quite a few motivational and inspirational speaking engagements. Some I found uplifting, some I found downright depressing.

The people who inspired me were the ones that, while sharing their challenging stories, also shared solutions they found throughout their journey and how their lives have changed for the better from the onset of what lead them to become inspirational speakers.

The speakers I found depressing were the ones that simply shared their sad tale. They told you what had happened to them to make their lives so difficult (all of these folks had a disability or catastrophic event happen to them of some sort), what their obstacles were and that's it. Very anticlimactic.

I don't know how the rest of the audience felt, but I am not inspired by simply hearing how difficult somebody else's life is, regardless of its level of challenge.

A disability or any dramatic life alteration does not automatically come with a license to inspire. I think some people feel it does. What inspires me is how an individual handles what happens to them. Do they play the victim role, "blah blah blah happened to me and I have no control over making things better," or the pity roll, "blah blah blah happened to me and I'm still here… Miserable, but here."

Okay, so this catastrophic event took place in your life, obviously extremely challenging. Then what? One person I went to hear left me so depressed after listening to him that I asked the event manager for my money back. I'm not kidding. I am going to spend an hour listening to a very sad man talk about how depressing his life is for $250.00? No way.

The incredible thing was, a few people heard me speak to the event manager. After listening to our exchange, they approached him as well and asked for their money back, too.

I understand challenging things happen to us all… I am writing this very article using Siri because I was in a car accident that paralyzed me from the shoulders down and I can't use my fingers to type… Believe me, I get it! But what are we going to DO about our challenging things?

How are we going to thrive (not survive, it's simply not enough) and feel fantastic, inside and out?! How do we smooth the bumps in the road for ourselves, or get help moving the mountains? To me, that's the definition of self-help and self im.

We are all works in progress. But it is the people sharing their challenges and their triumphs I find myself feeling full of hope and possibilities as I leave their seminar. Those are the folks who've moved me enough by their life's lessons, I want to apply them to my own.

If you're not able to attend a motivational or inspirational self-help lecture, no worries. Just take a good look around you. There are people jumping life's hurdles with grace, humor, dignity and even just plain fun right in your own backyard.

It's important to remember these people are not floating on an eternal silver-lined cloud, never experiencing trials and tribulations of their own. They are simply trying to find an easier, happier way through the muck that is in our way at times. And if one solution doesn't work, they try again. And sometimes again and again until their path is dry and muck free.

These folks also know one of the most important things about problem solving. If you don't do anything, one sure thing will happen... Nothing.

Winning The Lottery

One of the most challenging circumstances to be in life is to be stuck between a rock and a hard place. Or as I like to say, a rock and a rock.

Rocks possess not an ounce of give and keep you stuck exactly as you are. This is a scary place to be. How can you improve your circumstances if nothing can change? Whether it be finances, or relationships or work, if you have no options, where can you go? What can you do except to stay trapped?

You feel a loss of control, utterly helpless. You are a victim whose only hope of getting saved is by some random stroke of luck, such as winning the lottery or having someone come into your life and take care of all your challenges for you. So what is there to do except stay as you are, plod on, and accept this is just the way things are going to be.

At twenty-one years old, I won the lottery, but not the conventional kind with seven or eight digits to the left of the decimal point. Caught me completely by surprise, totally unexpected... what are the chances?! I am forty-one now. I can honestly say the last twenty years have been a life only imagined in my wildest dreams.

On February 7th, 1994, two of my girlfriends and I were on our way out for a fun night on the town when suddenly, we were in a car accident. It resulted in me sustaining a broken neck and a spinal cord injury, which would paralyze me for the rest of my life. As I laid in the hospital, initially on a respirator, slowly learning what it meant to have a spinal cord injury, I felt a rock and a rock settle themselves around me. Boulders, more like.

How would it be possible for me to have any type of meaningful life like this? I had control over nothing. I couldn't move my body, I couldn't feel my body, I couldn't feed myself, my voice was a whisper, I couldn't even go to the bathroom by myself. And this injury was permanent.

The medical community just didn't know how to fix me, and they still don't. The thought of one day looking back on my life and feeling it was miserable because I spent most of it in a wheelchair terrified me more than anything.

Even more so than my actual injury. I had absolutely no wish to simply be a survivor. I had to be a thriver. I was an all or nothing girl. I always had been and this injury did not change that. With no control over anything, how was I going to be me? I was in a dark place, and at times, I felt the panic rise up in me so powerful I was sure I would simply cease to exist.

Somewhere in those dark hours, a miracle occurred. Out of nowhere, a voice in my head told me I had still had choices. I had to have the courage to change my perception to see them, but they were there and they were endless. That realization is the lottery that came out of nowhere and saved my life.

Today, twenty years later, I lead a happy, healthy, busy, interesting life, filled with people I love and who love me. Do I go through challenging times? Absolutely. Do I still feel between a rock and a rock at times? Absolutely. But I know there are always choices I can make to change my circumstances for the better.

The bigger the challenge, the harder it is to see the choices. But knowing they are there, I look until I find them. My biggest challenges in life stems from issues related to being dependent on a wheelchair. But everyone has challenges they deal with every day.

Mine may be easier to imagine because my wheelchair is easy to see, it's in your face. But what's your wheelchair?

SPA

For most of us, today's lifestyle requires the pace of an Olympic runner. This seems to be especially true in the day of the life of a parent. I do not have children of my own, but I have been a close observer for thirty years of family members who do. I give them gold medals for keeping their sanity intact.

Before I became an aunt, which is when my real opportunity to become an observer began, I naïvely thought parents would be busiest when their children were little. But it seemed the older the kids became, the busier the parents became.

In retrospect, I believe I expected this because the younger children are, the less they can do for themselves. But this also means the younger children are, the less activities they are involved in. The kids in my family currently range from ages four to nineteen. Not only do some of them have a more hectic schedule then me, they have a more hectic schedule than their parents.

Kids over the age of four should come with their own driver. There is the regular shuttling to soccer practice, dance class, swim practice, sewing school, cub scouts, track practice, karate, tutors, orthodontist appointments…and I know I am only naming a small handful. Many parents perform this driving magic act while juggling a career, too.

While I applaud the parents contending with a hectic lifestyle, every person I know leads a very hectic lifestyle. I hear the same issue from friends coast to coast… Too much to accomplish and not enough time to accomplish it in.

We multi-task using cell phones, iPads, ipods, fax machines, email, texting, laptops, Skype, how-to videos online, credit cards, bank cards, online banking and atm's, all in a vain attempt to accomplish as much as we can as fast as we can.

But many times we fall short. It is in this "falling short" when we really feel the stress of our fast paced lives. If we could actually accomplish what we unrealistically and unfairly expect of ourselves in the time we allow, we would feel satisfied and gratified at the end of each day.

Instead, we feel more overwhelmed and at times, even disappointed in ourselves. In an already stressful, hectic life, these are not the emotions we need to be feeling in order to propel us toward accomplishing our goals and dreams.

Being an individual living with a disability requiring me to need assistance with 90% of my daily activities, I can get seriously frustrated about my own "daily to do list". Especially when you consider accomplishing our larger goals hinges directly on accomplishing our smaller, daily goals.

So how can we better manage our goals and responsibilities and still keep our sanity? I have come up with a little diddy I use called SPA. Simplify, Prioritize, Assistance. When I'm feeling harried, overwhelmed and *seriously* thinking of overdosing on mini cans of diet Pepsi's, I do my best to remember SPA.

First I simplify. I take a minute to look at each item on my daily to – do list. I see if I can make them easier working *smarter not harder* by managing my time wisely. I concentrate on making the most of the time I allotted for each task so I can move to the next task quickly.

It's also important to me to actually *enjoy* the task I'm doing, regardless how ordinary it is. I've found the best way to do this is *focus*. If I'm doing something mundane, like making a grocery list, but thinking about the cup of tea I promised myself as a reward for making the grocery list, I guarantee I won't enjoy my cup of tea.

Instead, I'll miss the enjoyment of my reward because I'll be thinking about the next task I have to do. Lots of going through the motion and little of enjoying the experience, or even experiencing the experience.

Next. Prioritize. What on your list can wait until later in the day or tomorrow, and what *must* get done today. You'll find the sooner you accomplish the things you feel are most important, even if they are not your favorite things to do, the easier and more enjoyable the rest of your tasks become.

Last. Assistance. Learn to recognize when you need help and then *ask for it.* If you possess the Superman or Wonder Woman complex and find this concept *extremely* difficult, think of a friend or family member who you would be happy to help out in a pinch and then ask away.

People need people, it's that simple. Assure the person you ask for help to call upon you when they are in need. They may have a hard time asking for help, as well. You initiating the request will show them it's okay not to be able to do everything on your own.

Losing Your Disability Virginity

If you are an individual living with a disability, it can be hard to meet new people and make friends. I've lived without a disability and I've lived with a disability and trust me, it's harder to make friends living with the latter. Why is this?

People meet at work, through social gatherings and mutual friends. They introduce themselves, shake hands and chat a bit. If they find each other interesting, they may make plans to meet again. This is the ABC's of starting a friendship.

But what if you are disabled and find people avoid you? When you're at a party, you get very limited eye contact and nobody is interested in shaking your hand. If you happen to get a conversation started with someone, you find them surveying the room, hoping to find another person to talk to. If these are your circumstances, it's going to be nearly impossible to make friends.

Having lived life on either side of the able-bodied and disabled fence, if you have a disability, I think 90% of the people you come in contact with have good intentions and are interested in getting to know you, just as they would want to get to know anybody. But they are nervous about their approach.

So if you happen to be a disability virgin, and have yet to break your ice with an individual who is disabled, allow me to give you a few pointers.

* People with disabilities realize a person who is introducing them-selves may be nervous. Let the disabled person be your guide. One of the first things people do upon introduction is shake hands. If the dis-abled person is not extending their hand and you are unsure if they are waiting for you or if they are physically unable to shake hands, lean-ing down to give a kiss on the cheek is perfectly appropriate.

* Assume nothing. Everyone with a disability has different capabili-ties. With me, I can extend my arm but cannot grip well with my fingers, especially on my right hand, which is usually the hand you extend upon meeting someone. I, instead, extend my left, and if the person falters a bit, a smile from me goes a long way in putting them at ease.

* Make an effort to be at the disabled person's physical level. Even if you are only being introduced, leaning down as you do so goes a long way in a disabled person's eyes. It shows you are aware enough to come off your height ladder and be in their chair for a moment. Don't misunderstand… Height ladders and wheelchairs are nobody's fault, but it is nice to be met in the middle by the person who has the capa-bility to do so.

24

* Don't ask how the individual became disabled. Many people are introduced to me, say hello and follow it with, "What happened to you?" I find that to be extremely rude, so I answer with, "I stubbed my toe." People are not sure how to react to this, and I usually get a confused look as they find an excuse to move away from me as soon as possible.

People need to understand how a person became disabled is a very personal thing. While the disabled individual may be accepting and socially adjusted to their disability now, they certainly were not in the beginning. Sustaining a permanent disability is a very grave loss. Asking them how it came to be is asking them to go back to a very painful place.

* If you're having your first conversation with a disabled person, introductions are over and the two of you have decided to get to know each other a bit. Do exactly that... Get to know the person. Don't ask questions that you wouldn't want someone to ask you. We earn the right to get to know each other more intimately as we put time in to develop a friendship.

* Be politically correct. An individual may say something to me regarding disabilities and not use the best choice of words. If someone corrects you and educates you on the appropriate word or phrase that should be used when referring to disabilities, simply apologize and thank them for letting you know. Any person with a disability you are having a pleasant conversation with will realize you were not trying to offend them, you simply did not know the difference. I use incorrect words all the time and I'm thankful when someone corrects me.

* If the disabled person you are speaking with is struggling to get something or do something, offer to help. They will appreciate you stepping up and not ignoring what they are trying to do. This does not mean you should hover or offer to do every little thing for a disabled person. This is another circumstance where you should let the disabled person be your guide.

Okay, I've given you a few pointers I hope you find useful. Meeting people you have things in common with and can form a friendship with is a rare thing for all of us. First impressions on both sides mean a lot in getting a friendship started. We should do everything we can to put our best foot forward.

Mandela Unconquered

At times, I find it hard to be inspired. Regardless of the constant sources of it around me, my perception will be skewed and I just can't feel it. This can happen when I am going through a particular challenging time. I'm frustrated, have lost a little hope perhaps, in need of a new solution for an old problem...you know those times, right?

With Nelson Mandela's passing, his life story was continually in the news. I was reminded of his astonishing accomplishments, all of which include an element of peace and equality for humanity. What amazes me the most, however, is he had time to accomplish what he did despite the fact he spent twenty-seven years in prison. Although he lived until he was ninety-five, almost a third of his life was spent locked in a cell.

To achieve all that he did, I think Nelson Mandela must have been constantly inspired. Since he was human, I'm guessing he experienced feelings of fear and doubt at times throughout his life, but I feel he possessed some continual river of inspiration...Something innate within him.

His inspiration may have been a only a trickle at times, depending on what he was experiencing, but it never dried up. How do you explain coming out of prison after twenty-seven years with as much, or perhaps even more, purpose and passion for your cause then when you went in. Purpose and passion to prove change can be achieved through respect and peaceful resistance, no less... Not war and vengeance.

I am always fascinated to know what moves people who accomplish core shaking, positive global change with their time on earth. My niece reminded me of the poem Nelson Mandela had with him in prison and that he gave it credit for his survival during those long years. I knew a few lines by heart, but not in its entirety. As I took the time to read it, to me, the poem clearly mirrored South Africa's beloved Madiba's own character.

Out of the night that covers me,
Black as the pit from pole to pole,
I thank whatever gods may be
For my unconquerable soul.

In the fell clutch of circumstance
I have not winced nor cried aloud.
Under the bludgeoning's of chance
My head is bloody, but unbowed.

Beyond this place of wrath and tears
Looms but the Horror of the shade,
And yet the menace of the years
Finds and shall find me unafraid.

It matters not how strait the gate,
How charged with punishments the scroll,
I am the master of my fate:
I am the captain of my soul.

~ Invictus, by William Ernest Henley.

Invictus is the Latin word for unconquered. Individuals who grace our planet, go through incredible suffering, then promote change through only peaceful means, all for their love of the greater good, will never cease to amaze me. Their spirit is eternally Invictus.

What I Am Thankful For

I am thankful for Thanksgiving Day 2013. I shared a beautiful Thanksgiving dinner at the Mohonk Mountain House with my mom and My Mike. Their annual buffet feast was fantastic. The food was excellent, the maître d' remembered us from last year and gave us VIP treatment. We had a gorgeous, panoramic view of the Catskill Mountain Range and the sun was shining.

I am thankful for my home. Not does it only provide a warm, dry roof over my head, but it is my very own little haven I share with My Mike, my animals and my family. It is filled with peace, love and inspiration, mixed in with A LOT of necessary silliness.

I am thankful for the children in my life. They are my greatest inspiration and provide me with a never ending pool of topics to write about. They are my greatest joy.

I am thankful for my childhood. It was a bit challenging due to a lack of financial resources and parents who divorced. It taught me independence, the importance of living within your means, strive to improve your circumstances, the importance of communication and the consequences of the lack of it. It instilled in me there is something to be said for doing the right thing. It's when my extreme love of animals began because we lived on a horse farm that came with cows, goats, chickens, cats and a dog.

I am thankful for my spinal cord injury. It has taught me patience and the importance of experiencing joy wherever you can. It has allowed the children in my life to experience firsthand that different is only that... Different.

I am thankful for the countless doctors and their teams who, over the years, have taken such extraordinary care of me under perilous circumstances and have saved my life more then once. They have enhanced my quality of life by helping me get rid of pain through the magic touch of gifted surgeons and the healing touch of their teams as I recovered.

I am thankful for the countless people in the medical industry, from doctors to nurses aides, who tried to give me less care than I deserved. They reiterated the power of self advocacy, that everybody deserves to be accommodated and never to settle for less than you need.

I am thankful for my community. It offered a picturesque, friendly, safe place to grow up. I never remember locking our house or car doors when I was a kid, and you could wander away from your mom at the grocery store without her having to panic. As an adult, my community has been continually supportive towards myself and my family as we live with a spinal cord injury.

I am thankful for my relentlessness. It has taught me to push myself beyond society's comfort zone in how a person with a disability should lead their life. I lead the life I wish to lead, regardless of public opinion or popularity. My relentlessness has also taught me the consequences of pushing too hard when instead, I should have exercised patience.

I am thankful for my independence. It was instilled in me as a child if you desire something, you had to go out and get it; somebody else wasn't going to get it for you. I learned I had the power to get what I wished and make things happen by simply following through with the steps to do so. When I became disabled, my strong sense and need for independence carried me far, and will continue to do so my entire life.

I am thankful for all the places my life has led me. I have met extraordinary people throughout my travels, both near and far. Some encounters were brief, others will last a lifetime.

I am thankful for my country. My country allows me the right to speak my opinion, beliefs and thoughts freely, without the worry of political persecution. My country allows me to be me.

I am thankful for My Mike. My life partner through good and bad, he is my first line of defense against the despair I sometimes feel. He offers continued love, acceptance and support. He has the ability to make me feel tomorrow will be better if today was quite a challenge. He is forever my fellow Titan.

Lastly, I am thankful for my family, blood related and beyond. You show continuous unconditional love by supporting me in my life choices, even when you don't agree with them. As a unit, you have allowed me to borrow your will to move forward when I have had none left of my own. You share your lives and your children with me as if they were mine. For Thanksgiving and always, I give you all that I am and all that I hope to be. Without you, my spirit would have ceased to exist a long time ago. You have all my love always.

PNN...Positive News Network

While I think it's important to stay abreast of the current events going on in our world, I am not a big fan of the news. At all. I went through almost a decade of refusing to watch one minute of news, nor would I allow anyone in my house to watch it. I found it extremely depressing, unbearably redundant and strangely addictive. Like a car wreck you couldn't look away from. I figured if there was something serious enough going on in the world, I was sure to hear about it from somebody.

In the last few years, I have mellowed some. I'll watch a little CNN to get a fifteen minute catch up on events around the globe and I like "Nightly News with Brian Williams" on NBC at 6:30 PM. Rather, I like Brian Williams... He comes into our living room in the evening with an energy and grace that makes me feel he genuinely cares about the stories he is reporting on, and he seems as unbiased as humanly possible. To be fair, I have the feeling most journalists care about the stories they are reporting on, but thirty minutes with Brian is about all the news I can take in one dose.

In his thirty minute broadcast, there are about twenty-three minutes of actual news. The remaining seven minutes are broken up into commercial breaks. The very last story every evening is called "Making A Difference." This segment of the program is always about an inspiring person or organization doing wonderful, selfless acts to make the world a better place. Many times, I am moved to tears by these stories and motivated to do more in my own life to help my fellow human being.

The story lasts somewhere between two and three minutes, and then Brian Williams bids you good night. Prior to that, the first twenty minutes, 99.9% of the time, are stories of school shootings, the latest tragedy Mother Nature has bestowed upon us, the nasty negatives of politics, the latest war(s) casualties, terrorism, our stuttering economy... I could go on forever.

If only three out of the twenty-news minutes of news reported has an inspiring, feel-good, uplifting nature, we are watching 92% of negative and 8% of positive. That's like a diet of 92% carbs and 8% of fruits and vegetables. Who could live a long, happy, healthy life with a diet like that?

I realize I am doing a bit of generalizing by using only one program on one network as an example, but I've watched dozens of other network news programs and I found them all to be pretty much the same... Depressing, redundant and addictive, with each network having an occasional uplifting exception. So what is there to do? Who holds the power to change things? The networks, the journalists or us, the viewers?

Has society become so addicted to tragedy and trauma that the news programs purposely make it the majority of what they air because that's what sells? And what about copycat crimes? I don't think it's a coincidence when you hear of multiple mass shootings within a week or ten days... Ideas are given from television.

What if we tried something. What if there was a news network that only reported on inspiring, uplifting, motivating stories? It could be called PNN... Positive News Network. It would broadcast stories about Doctors Without Borders, parents who are homeschooling their children and getting them into college by the age of twelve (true story), incredible animals that reside in Africa, the stunning glaciers in Alaska, hearing politicians speak of hope, growth and change and then putting their words into action, a country previously under a dictatorship that has just become a democracy... as with the negative, I could go on and on about the positive.

Imagine the copycat "crimes" we may see from people watching twenty-three minutes of PNN. Someone may join the Peace Corps, or take steps to live a "greener" life to preserve Mother Nature, or register to vote for the first time or become more involved in their child's education. Yes, I could go on forever.

More interestingly, how would we feel after watching twenty-three minutes of news stories like that. I feel happy just writing about it. Imagine actually experiencing it, and after the program was over, you would be left thinking of all the incredible, inspiring things happening around our globe instead of wondering how so many tragic events continue to occur.

I'm not so naïve that if PNN (or a network like it) existed, the world's population would flock to it and never watch another regular news program again. I do think there is something to be said for staying in touch with what is happening around us, and beautiful events occur along with catastrophic ones. But what if we changed our diet a bit?

Not too radical, not overnight, but what if we made things slightly more balanced... Say 80% CNN and 20% PNN. Would we change, or would we stay exactly the same? It's like Nature vs. Nurture... Is it genetic inheritance or environmental exposure that develops and determine who we are?

Since I can't do anything about my genetics but I can do something about my choice of television programs, I'm going to pray Turner Broadcasting launches it's sister station, PNN... Positive News Network. At the very least, a few more servings of fruits and vegetables every day wouldn't hurt any of us.

Chapter 2:
A DAY IN THE LIFE OF SCI

The Top Five Most Fabulous Things About Having A Spinal Cord Injury

Twenty years ago, if someone told me I would experience fabulous things due to my spinal cord injury, I would have punched them in the face. Actually, I would have hired someone to do it for me, as my newly paralyzed arm could not. But you get my meaning.

In all honesty, there were a few people in my very close circle who told me this (phrased a bit differently at the time... I don't remember the word fabulous being used.) I didn't possess any desire to punch them, as I knew what they said came from a loving place. It was just unfathomable to me at the time.

Plain and simple, they were right. More than right. I would accept a cure for SCI yesterday if it were available. But I would not trade the experiences I've had and the positive ripple effect that will grow with younger generations my injury has influenced the last twenty years for gold.

After the first most fabulous item on my list, the rest are in no particular order. They are all equally fabulous, fantastic and simply special in my heart.

1. My kids. I won't be a parent in this lifetime. I am lucky enough, however, to have seven nieces and nephews my family generously shares with me since each were born.

The two oldest are the only ones who experienced me both uninjured and injured. I babysat them constantly for more than a decade before my injury. After my injury, they assured me they would now take care of me.

The other five range in age from four to nineteen. My disability is not an issue for them. They grew up with me needing help with certain things and that's just the way it was.

From the moment they were born, I helped them understand we could play and do anything they wanted... we may just do it differently. They could care less. If only adults were that accepting.

I have an opportunity to instill in these precious human beings different is just different, and it's nothing to be feared. They will become adults with this idea and be able to influence the world how our differences are to be accepted and embraced, not judged and ridiculed.

I've experienced plenty of fear-based ridicule and judgment due to my disability. I thank God every single day I can continue to influence these wonderful children. They will use their voices in their own generation regarding the need for social acceptance.

2. People I meet. I have met some of the most incredible people that are true humanitarians. Surgeons with hearts of gold and hands of magic. Hospital staff from the best institutions in the world to clinics in third world countries, all taking care of you as if you were their own family.

True hands on healers, living in extremely modest surroundings, in countries whose languages I did not speak, who charged not a dime but only wanted to share their gift. Folks like me, traveling the world, seeking emotional healing as much as physical. So many strangers who have done me a kindness throughout my life's journey. Lifelong friendships made during my travels. The valuable lesson of people need people.

3. Paralyzed perks. Disabled parking rocks, especially in bad weather and when you are trying to get to a movie on time.
My niece and nephew went *crazy* at Disney World when they realized wheelchair folks go to the front of the line. *And* can go on rides multiple times, without having to get off. I must admit, the Disney World perks were a lot of fun for us adults, too.

Shoes. I am a shoe freak. I can't walk, so even if I buy cheap shoes, they always look new. That doesn't mean I don't buy new shoes... it means I have a hundred pair. At least.

4. Being treated the same. I have a wonderful, supportive, unconditional loving family. They have big hearts and some of them have even bigger mouths. And they give me absolutely no special treatment due to my disability.

If I try to play the disabled card to manipulate one of them, it has absolutely zero effect. I wouldn't have it any other way.

5. Opportunity for awareness. There is so much negative stereotyping regarding disabled individuals. People meet me and say how pretty I am. A spinal cord injury paralyzes you. It doesn't smash you against the ugly tree.

Some folks talk really loud when they meet me. A spinal cord injury paralyzes you, it doesn't make you deaf. Or mute. Or blind. Or stupid.

I realize people do not know what your issues are when you are disabled. Here is a revolutionary idea. Assume nothing. Actually take the time to observe and get to know the disabled individual for thirty seconds or so. You will quickly see how their disability affects them.

The fact I am in a position to draw awareness to end the stereotyping of our fellow humans based on how they *look* and instead, get to know their moral character is a gift from my injury. I pray with my whole heart I make an impact on this issue in my lifetime.

So there you have it. My top five most fabulous things about being injured. There are many, many more, but you would be reading forever.

Dining Out Disabled

My boyfriend and I are guilty of being food snobs. One of our favorite things to do is go out to dinner at a fantastic restaurant that offers superb food, an eclectic wine list and excellent service.

Since the fabulous ADA guidelines make ramps required at commercial buildings, logistically, there should not be any problems eating at restaurants, right? Keep reading.

First of all, the word logistics in all its forms does not apply to anything regarding the ADA. Logistics implies coordination, planning and strategy. I have experienced nothing of the kind when it comes to the ADA.

A perfect example. The restaurant My Mike and I arrive at has a ramp. Great, I can get inside! What else could possibly be needed for us to enjoy our evening?

Tables. Most restaurant tables are not wheelchair friendly. What do I mean? How can a table pose a problem?

First, the height. If a table is too low, my knees hit it and I cannot get underneath. I am tall, so I am dealing with at least a foot and a half of space between my abdomen and the table. Who can reach their food and drink sitting that far away?

Second, the legs. Most restaurant table legs are designed in such a way they cause the same problem the table height does. I cannot get close enough to the table because my wheelchair wheels or knees or foot rests hit the table legs.

If the table has a pedestal in the middle, I hit the pedestal before I'm close enough to the table to eat. If the table legs branch out like a spider, my wheels hit them, causing the same problem.

Here is where it becomes interesting. I refuse to not be accommodated in a situation like this. I am asking for a table I can eat a meal at comfortably... not for an elevator to be instantly constructed in a sixty year old five-story walk up.

The restaurant has a disabled sticker displayed in its window, right alongside its Zagat's sticker. They need to live up to their advertisement and be truly accessible.

When we are shown by the maître d' to an unfriendly wheelchair table, I quietly explain my needs to him. When this happens, My Mike is already surveying the room for a workable table.

Some proprietors are fantastic. They profusely apologize. They want me to show them exactly what I need. They promise to find something I will be completely comfortable with.

Some proprietors are jerk offs. They show us what they have to offer, and if it doesn't work, that's my problem. I am sure to tell these types of folks that neither myself nor any of my family will ever grace their establishment again.

They rarely care about this. What they do not realize yet, however, is many of my family members enjoy wining and dining at fine restaurants in our area on a very regular basis. I throw a few names over my shoulder as I leave, and I have seen more then one restaurant owner have an "Uh-Oh " look come across their face.

The funny thing is, if a restaurant is willing to work with me, 90% of the time we can figure out a table arrangement I am comfortable with. It's not rocket science. It's called caring.

Going out to dinner is supposed to help you decompress, not add on more stress. In an effort to accomplish this, if we are going to a restaurant for the first time, I explain my needs when I make our reservation.

Some people start talking extremely loud as soon as they hear the word wheelchair. Thanks for shouting. I was worried I wouldn't be able to hear you because of my paralysis.

Some folks cannot grasp the table situation, but promise to do whatever is necessary when we arrive. Some live up to their promise. Others find it too difficult to deal with.

Occasionally, people understand exactly what I need. When we arrive at the restaurant, there is a wheelchair friendly table waiting for us, with a smile from the maître d'.

We have acquired a few favorite restaurants. The food is fantastic every time we go. The employees are pleasant and take the time to get to know you so they remember what you like. There is a candlelit table waiting for us in a great location of the restaurant. And it is perfectly wheelchair friendly.

Days of Summer

Life doesn't get much better than this…It's Labor Day, and I am at my boyfriend's dad's house, sitting next to the pool. It's 82°, the humidity is low and the cloudless sky is a crystal clear, deep blue.

I would call this an L.A. sky. I lived in L.A. for five years. It seemed every day Mother Nature made a deep, blue sky that made you dizzy if you looked at it too long. It was so clear you felt as if you were looking into forever.

Back to Labor Day. The warm, dry breeze occasionally blows my hair in my eyes, obscuring my vision as I wrote from my beloved Mac. Every so often, I turned my face upward to feel the warmth of the sun.

My boyfriend recently noticed my computer battery getting low and knowing my love of this glorious weather, he ran an extension cord from the pool cabana to my laptop so I could stay on my prime real estate.

A few family and friends were over to enjoy the day with us. We were barbecuing, cocktailing and listening to a fantastic array of tunes, courtesy of my nephew's iPod. I close my eyes, take a deep breath and exhale.

My body felt great. The warm, dry weather took all of my aches and pains away. I also had a yummy, contented feeling we experience in our gut when the moment we are in is, quite simply, perfect.

I'm constantly and continually amazed how quickly time goes by. These glorious days of summer seemingly just start, and suddenly, they come to a close. Before we know it, Jack Frost appears for the first time of the season, marking the point of no return for summer.

I cringe a bit, (okay, a lot!), at the thought of the Northeast winter, filled with turtlenecks, snow tires and frigid temperatures with the possibility of acute frostbite. Every year, as summer closes and winter approaches, I wonder how I will fare.

I remind myself there is a flipside to everything... even winter. Shopping for cozy, soft sweaters, trips to our favorite coffee house in the snow for a Chai Tea Latte. The likely hood of my boyfriend snuggling with me more than usual to keep me warm...

There is a positive aspect to every negative one. It is so important for each of us to recognize this. We can all be guilty of not seeing the positive at times, but many people in society constantly choose to focus on the negative instead of the positive.

These people are emotional vampires. After spending time with a chronically negative person, I feel as if the blood and energy has been sucked from my body.

I certainly go through times when all I can see in a certain set of circumstances are the negative parts. But the difference between me and an emotional vampire is my negative outlook is temporary.

At some point, I choose to change my perception. I shake off the negative, and look for the positive. If I can't find some positive, I create some.

With time flying as fast as it does, not recognizing the positive facets of our experiences is simply wasting our lives. To me, this is one of the scariest thoughts in my life. Correction... The scariest thought.

To look back on times in my life and have memories of misery are such a waste. Imagine being in the winter years of your life. Looking back on your life's journey, the majority of what you feel is negative thoughts and regret. Even writing it gives me goose bumps.

If we make the choice to try and focus on the positive of everything we experience, our memories will be filled with joyous moments. We will still remember challenging times and sadness. We are human and all works in progress. But we will know we did our best to find the sunshine.

The dis-Ability Of Intimacy, Love and Sex

Marvin Gaye says it best when his voice croons, "Sexual healing is something that's good for me…" In my opinion, it's not only something that is good for him; it's something that is good for you, for me, for everybody.

Intimacy, love and sex are three key ingredients for an individual to experience a happy life. Everybody needs to be nurtured, encouraged, supported, and allowed to express themselves sexually. Sharing this with someone you care for is something I believe all humans are meant to experience.

Sustaining a spinal cord injury paralyzed me physically; it did not paralyze my need and desire for love and sex. If anything, it magnified it. Let's be honest. There aren't too many things better than spending intimate time with your partner when you are feeling bad and need a boost in spirit.

In the word "intimate," I am encompassing sex and love and all that's in between. And why the majority of society thinks having a disability goes hand in hand with losing their desire for love and sex is something I do not understand.

Sex is a hot topic, regardless of age, social standing or physical ability. When one of my nephew's was about seven, he brought up the subject of sex to me. Before I gave an explanation, I asked him what he thought it was. He said it was when two people got naked, stood really close together and then kissed. Since he was on the right track, I agreed with him and let it go at that.

When one of my niece's was seven, (must be the childhood form of the seven year itch), told me her neighbor woke up one morning with

40

a big belly that had just "popped" with a baby now in it. "That happens sometimes, Aunt Amy...People who aren't married just 'pop.'"

I tried to explain that's not *exactly* what happens. As I attempted to clarify, at a seven-year-old's level, how a baby gets into a woman's belly, my niece looked at me as if I had three heads.

She traded embarrassing looks with a friend she was with. She proceeded to tell me I had no idea what I was talking about and I better be sure to talk to my boyfriend to get a better understanding of how babies are made.

When you are an individual living with a disability, curiosity about sex doesn't stop with children. I've found adults to be even more inquisitive, with a few distinct differences. The innocent, questioning mind of a child is replaced by the rude nosiness of an adult.

Since being injured, dozens of total strangers have come right up to me and asked, "Excuse me, but I was just wondering, can you have sex?" Or better yet, "Excuse me, I don't mean to be rude, but *how* do you have sex?" Strangers even asked me this while I was still in ICU immediately following my injury.

Twenty years post injury, I have a few short, sweet, remarks to put people in their place. I didn't, however, have this ability at first. Initially, before any emotional healing regarding my sexuality had taken place, thoughtless questions from strangers regarding my sex life were devastating to me.

It's not easy for anybody to meet society's expectations of attractiveness in today's world. Placing a body that functions differently into the expectation equation doesn't make it any easier.

In every TV commercial, magazine, and billboard promoting everything from clothing to suitcases, from home improvements to spring water, people in the advertisements are thin where they should be, thick where they should be and perfectly groomed. While I was *extremely* curious about how sex would be post injury, I was also terrified.

I had no way of knowing how my body was going to respond to different types of sexual stimulation or what I would be able to feel. And while I still felt sexual desire, I did not know if a man would find me sexually desirable.

Even though I now possess quick responses to rude questions regarding my sexuality, the person asking me does not know this. They do not know I am seasoned from two decades of rude questions from individuals like themselves. It could be my first time out in society since getting injured.

Does a person honestly think the selfish need to satisfy their curiosity justifies a hurtful, unkind level of rudeness? I find this to be one of the most unjustified levels of self entitlement.

I believe it is human nature to be curious; we all are. But does that mean I have the right to approach a woman standing in line at the movies with her family and ask, "Excuse me, but are your very large breasts real or implants? Do they prevent you from sleeping on your stomach?" In these instances, it seems self entitlement overrides common decency.

Life is messy. And so is sex, whether you are disabled or not. Educate yourself on how your body works and be honest with your partner about any special needs you may have.

If you find yourself thinking about your own desire for sexual healing, good for you. Regardless of your physical ability or disability, think about how your current sexuality makes you feel. Sometimes what we wish to experience or thought what we were experiencing and the reality of what *is* are two very different things.

If this is true for you in the intimacy, love and sex areas of your life, know you can do something about it. Take a deep breath and step through your fear. By just doing that, you will feel empowered and exhilarated, and on your way to feeling stimulated and invigorated. Why would we want to feel anything but?

Oh My God! Your Wheelchair Is On Fire!

I smelled smoke, but it was so faint, I couldn't be sure. I asked my friend Andrea if she smelled something burning, and she said she was just about to ask me the same thing. Within seconds, the smell was getting stronger. It was the acrid smell of wires burning. "Oh my God!" Andrea suddenly gasped. "Your wheelchair is on fire!"

I am blessed with a very supportive family, immediate and extended. When I was initially injured, I was in the hospital a total of six months. The first three of those months were spent in an acute care facility, and the last three months were spent in a rehabilitation center. Regardless of the two hour commute to both hospitals, my family made sure I had a visitor every single day.

Acute care's job was to get you stable enough for a rehab center. The rehab's job was to get you physically strong and emotionally prepared to live as independent as possible when you transition home. This not only included physical and occupational therapy, but also classes my family and I attended to learn how a spinal cord injured body worked. The rehab center very much encouraged family and friends to take an inclusive, hands-on attitude as we experienced this hairpin turn in the road together.

I was sitting in occupational therapy on one of the countless days my dear friend Andrea came to visit. We had learned transfer training the week before, and today our goal was for her and I to get it down pat together. My OT instructor was right by our sides, guiding, spotting, encouraging and praising us.

Andrea and I accomplished it a few times successfully, with each time getting easier and less scary for both of us. Andrea had transferred me in my wheelchair for the third time when my OT told us to take a break while she went and assisted somebody else. She could tell we were eager to continue, but we promised not to try anything without her standing by.

Andrea was sitting on the blue exercise mat and I in my wheelchair when I initially smelled smoke. It was very faint at first, just a whiff or two and then nothing. But within only the matter of a few seconds, not only did Andrea and I notice it, but other patients and staff were commenting on it as well. It smelled like burning rubber or wires.

Suddenly, Andrea cried, "Aim, your wheelchair is on fire!" I could now see the smoke rising from under my chair and people around me were gasping and scattering. I thought I was going to be engulfed in flames.

Two therapists moved in lightning speed. One transferred me onto an exercise mat as the other put the wheelchair joystick in high gear and ran alongside the chair to get it out of the building as quickly as possible. Luckily, there was an emergency exit about twenty feet away from us and the wheelchair was quickly outside.

Once outside, we could really see how badly the wheelchair was smoking and there were flames licking out from underneath. Andrea and I were dumbfounded. We were nervous enough when we started our transfer training… Good thing we did not know I was sitting on a ticking time bomb.

Every single staff person was utterly shocked. Some of them had thirty years of OT experience, and even they had never seen or heard of anything like this ever happening. You can bet all of the patients were looking at the brand of wheelchair they were sitting in. If it was the same brand they witnessed starting an electrical fire all on its own, they wanted out. Immediately. Who could blame them?

Physically, I was fine. Emotionally, I was not. I had never felt so trapped and helpless in my entire life, and I refused to sit in a power wheelchair for years. Unfortunately, this was much to my detriment. I should have gotten right back on the horse.

A power wheelchair does more than give you the independence to move around as you wish. It also has the capability to reposition you in such a way that allows blood flow to the areas of your body that take the brunt of pressure from sitting constantly. Blood flow and circulation allows your skin and tissue to stay healthy.

I paid a high price many times for not using a power wheelchair. It could have prevented me from countless circumstances of suffering. I finally had to face my fear and get beyond it or I was not going to live a long, healthy life. When it was presented to me this way, by a world class surgeon I loved and respected, the choice was easy.

Today, I am happy to say I cannot imagine a life without the independence and health a power wheelchair provides. My only regret is I didn't face my fear sooner. It's incredible how much suffering we sometimes put ourselves through before common sense kicks in.

The Hitman

We've all experienced road rage. Either you yourself are a mad dash driver and cannot stand slow drivers and traffic hangups or, you've been a passenger of a road rage driver. Regardless of how much of a rush you are in, sometimes you just have to wait your turn. Especially if you find yourself at a red light and you need to make a left turn.

When I lived in LA, I was in my early to mid twenties. A few of the good friends I made were on the UCLA track team. I lived in Brentwood and UCLA is in Westwood, the next town over. You could almost walk from one town to the other quicker then you could drive, if you included the time it took to find parking.

My track team friend Brady and I were walking back from Starbucks, on our way to campus. We were on the corner of Westwood Boulevard, which takes you straight to UCLA. The walkers had a green light and we started to cross. I was in my manual, lightweight wheelchair, and Brady was pushing me with one hand while holding our Starbucks tray in the other.

Out of the corner of my eye, I saw a car getting ready to make a left-handed turn. I figured the driver was going to crawl into the intersection as far as he could behind Brady and I as we crossed. By his speed, I quickly realized he had no plans of simply following us until we were out of his way. Instead, he whizzed around the front of us, and as he did, he clipped my chair and caused my back wheel to pop right off.

Had it not been for the strength and quick reaction of my friend, my body would have tumbled right onto the pavement. Brady somehow prevented my chair from tipping and scooped me up with the other. He got me and the remainder of my wheelchair onto the sidewalk. As we watched, my detached wheel rolled into the busy afternoon traffic and was smashed by a car.

Just as this was unfolding, friends of ours turned onto Westwood Boulevard and spotted us. Brady and I made an odd sight… He was holding me while also keeping one of his feet on the seat of my chair to keep it from rolling away from us. He couldn't reach down far enough to put the break on the chair with me in his arms.

Our friends zipped over to where we were. They had a convertible, and it was easy to plop me into a seat. Westwood Boulevard is filled with stoplights, and we could see the car that hit my wheelchair was stopped two lights ahead of us. Altogether, there were six of us, and we unanimously decided the person who had hit me needed to apologize to my face.

The "Hitman" had the bad luck of hitting a disabled person's wheelchair who had Olympic caliber male track athletes as friends. Two of my buddies took off like jackrabbits, caught up with the Hitman's car and yanked him out of it. After giving him a good shake and a couple of wallops, they pulled his car into a curbside parking space.

By this time, the car I was in had caught up with them. We pulled up next to the Hitman's car, and he apologized. Numerous times, as I remember, and he didn't need encouraging. I had a few choice praises of my own to say to him.

Now we had to deal with my broken wheelchair. We decided the Hitman should pay for the repair. We were lucky enough a nearby home health equipment store was open and by some miracle, had the type of wheel I needed in stock. Actually, what they had was another wheelchair exactly like mine, and they simply took a back wheel off it. My chair was fixed in five minutes.

I rode in my friend's convertible to the store, with the Hitman follow-ing us. My two friends who had chased the Hitman down accompanied him in his car so he wouldn't get lost, accidentally on purpose. The Hitman had to pay extra for my chair to be fixed imme-diately, as opposed to waiting a week for an ordered wheel. He didn't argue about any of it. With another few choice phrases from all of us, my friends and I parted ways with the Hitman in the home health equipment store parking lot.

All in all, it could've been much worse. My friend and I could've been hurt. I could've had to deal with a wheelchair that wasn't fixa-ble. Our other friends could've been going in the opposite direction, and poor Brady would've had to carry me quite a ways to get me to a safe seat.

But the worst thing would have been if my friends weren't fast on their feet. The Hitman could've gotten away without a good hearty shake, wallop and scare. I'll admit it… Revenge was sweet.

Excuse Me, I Was Just Wondering…Can You Have Sex?

Strangers ask me questions regarding my injury all the time. Some people approach me trepidatiously, others flag me down as if I had just left a party with their coat instead of mine. They ask what brand of wheelchair I have because they need one for a family member, friend, etc. If I'm getting out of my van, folks will ask me if it came modified for a wheelchair, how much did it cost, did insurance cover it… Same types of questions they ask about my wheelchair. Reasona-ble questions you could ask any stranger.

I'm happy to answer these questions. When you become disabled, you're not given a survival guide containing information that lets you know how to get the most out of your health insurance, how to apply for state and federal benefits, a list of organizations offering financial assistance for things you may need regarding home modifications, vehicle modifications, employment placement assistance and job training, home health aides, physical therapy and countless other services you may need.

Trying to research this type of information when you desperately need it is extremely stressful. You are not even sure what you are looking for, because there is no one to tell you what benefits and programs exist, what you may be eligible for and how to apply for them. You and your family also need advice as to what products and services will meet your needs better than others so you can spend your money and your health insurance limit wisely.

The very first van I had modified was a nightmare for me to ride in. We had no idea there was more than one way to modify a vehicle. We were under an extreme amount of stress, we needed a van as soon as possible and there was no one to inform us of our choices. Once you spend tens of thousands of dollars buying a vehicle and having it modified, you don't get to return it, say it doesn't fit, and get a different one that fits you better.

Being well informed is priceless. I am more than happy to share any practical information with someone, in the hopes of saving them some time, money and stress by not having to figure it out on their own. There are, however, questions I do mind being asked because they have nothing to do with practicality. They have to do with an individual's need for drama.

It would take a library of encyclopedias to contain all of the rude, inappropriate and thoughtless questions complete strangers have asked me over the years. The most outrageous one to date in my opinion is, "Excuse me, but I was just wondering… Can you have sex?" I'm curious how many Emily Post quotes there are regarding this topic.

I was standing in line with a few friends, waiting to get tickets for a movie. I could feel a woman's eyes on me from behind. I could partially see her because she was standing a bit to my side, not directly behind me. She was looking at me from head to toe and back again and whispering to the woman she was with.

I accept the fact that people are going to look at me. They are curious, I get it. I'll allow a look or two from someone, and when I make eye contact with them, I smile. 90% of the time, they smile back. But when the staring begins, so does the rudeness. Some folks have the decency to look away once they realize I've observed them staring at me… Others just keep right on staring.

I could see the woman leaning forward as she reached out to tap me on the shoulder. I turned my chair so I was directly in front of her. She raised an eyebrow as she took a step towards me and asked in a clear voice, "Excuse me, but I was just wondering… Can you have sex?"

The woman she was with looked mortified. Everyone standing in line was now staring at us because it was easy to hear what she had said. I looked her directly in the face and said, "I was actually wondering something about you. Are your very large breasts real?"

This woman happened to have breasts that looked like two canta-loupes strapped to her chest, resting just below her chin. They were very obvious implants. Somehow the Universe gave me the timing to have that comment in my head when I needed it. It's the worst feeling when you think of what you wanted to say in a situation, hours after it occurred.

It is none of my business how people surgically augment their bodies. It's their body, their business. Just like it's absolutely nobody's busi-ness regarding my sex life. My sex life, my business.

After I responded to the woman's question, everyone in line clapped. I turned around and continued to wait with my friends for our tickets. The woman and her friend left quickly, and although I was tempted, I didn't turn around to see them go.

I think some people feel just because they are curious about some-thing, it's okay to ask. Similar to a feeling of false entitlement. I see people every day I find curious and wonder certain things about them; sometimes personal things. I would never simply stride up, ask them something extremely personal and expect a sincere answer. I'm going to respect their right to privacy instead of fulfilling my desire of curiosity.

Mornings Can Be Rough

Mornings during the fall season are an amazing time. Nature's light is exquisite as it ever so slowly pulls back its curtain to reveal a new day. The freshness of the air smells better than clean laundry, and the dew sparkles on the grass and leaves, highlighting their brilliant range of colors. Mother Nature is effortlessly showing off.

I'd like to know her secret, because for me, mornings can be the toughest time of day. Regardless of what time I go to bed, in the morning, I rarely feel like I have had enough sleep.

The guilt factor generally makes it impossible for me to sleep in, because when I try, I generally lay in bed and think about everything I need to accomplish by the end of the day and how am I going to do it by laying in bed?! After twenty minutes of this, mixed with thoughts of "just close your eyes, just close your eyes and dose off", I give up, have a cup of coffee made and open my bedroom blinds.

My day has started, only now my coffee is topped off with a bit of anxiety because I feel as if I'm getting a late start. My body, not my personality, dictates how long my personal care will take, ie: bathing, dressing, etc.

People living with spinal cord injuries don't hop out of bed quite as quickly as an able-bodied person. After laying in bed with very little movement for eight hours, my body is very stiff. I feel like the tin man in "The Wizard of Oz"…I need an oil can with my cup of coffee.

I also get cold very easily, so pulling the covers back to start moving around is torture. My aide turns my bedroom thermostat to 80° twenty minutes before I need to start moving around. The girls who work with me wear shorts and a tank top in my house in the middle of February because my house temperature is usually set to "bake."

The entire process of me getting ready for my day and taking care of all my bodily needs can be anywhere from two to three hours. It is not only the outside of my body that is paralyzed but also the inside. I only have so much control over how fast the inside of my body moves. Ask anyone who has a spinal cord injury... Sometimes your body cooperates, and sometimes it goes completely berserk.

There are some mornings when I have a hard time opening my blinds and having my cup of coffee because the thought of going through the routine I have to in order to simply start my day is just too over-whelming. And that's just the beginning of my day.

Who's to say the rest of my day is filled with entirely fabulously fun things? Maybe it's a day I already know is filled with challenging things. That fact makes opening the blinds even harder.

Somewhere in these moments, I find myself shifting my thoughts to Mother Nature and her brilliant mornings. And regardless of what her day entails, we can count on her to open her blinds for us.

I feel my perception change with just that one thought, and instead of all the challenges that lay before me, I think of all the blessings I know I will experience that day. By now, I am smiling, my coffee has kicked in, my room is warm and I am ready to throw the covers back. Let the day begin!

The Top Five Things That Stink About Having A Spinal Cord Injury

You may automatically think not being able to walk is the worst thing about living with SCI. When I was first injured, I thought the same thing. Quickly, I learned that is not so by far. Not for me, anyway.

1. Being cold. Until I injured my spinal cord, I don't even think it oc-curred to me I had one. Brain, heart, lungs, kidneys... Those were the main organs you kept in mind. Interestingly enough, the spinal cord assist's in the functioning of all those organs except the brain. One thing our spinal cord does greatly affect is our hypothalamus, which

controls our body's ability to regulate temperature. Being spinal cord injured, my body is now like a reptile's. Whatever climate I am in, my body tries to achieve that temperature. And while 80° sounds warm, it is 18° below our bodies regular temperature of 98.6°. In a nutshell, I am constantly, painfully cold. The worst part is, once I get cold, it takes two to three hours for me to warm up, regardless if I am in a sauna.

2. Being hot. My injury has taken away my body's ability to sweat. During the summer months, I have to be extremely careful I do not overheat. It happens very quickly since my body cannot sweat to keep me cool. One summer I suffered from heatstroke and lost my ability to speak. This was very scary, the scariest part being how quickly it happened.

If I could change only one thing about my body, it would be my temperature regulation. When you are freezing, it's hard to enjoy what you are doing. When you need to keep yourself covered in ice packs and have to run from shady spot to shady spot, it's equally hard to enjoy what you are doing.

3. Finding good home help. When I was initially injured, I thought everyone who was a home health aide was going to be a version of Florence Nightingale or Clara Barton. Why else would you choose to take care of people?

Unfortunately, this is not the case. I have hired hundreds of girls to help me in my home. I phone screen them, I interview them face-to-face, I do background checks and I do extensive hands-on training. You may think at this point I would be a good judge (for want of a better word) of who would excel at being a home health aide and who would not. You may also think I was a good judge of character to feel who has good intentions and who does not.

I am not good at any of it. I have been left high and dry, with a "no call, no show" from staff. I've been verbally and physically abused from staff. I've had things stolen from my home a thousand times. All of this done by individuals I thought were going to be fabulous employees.

4. Urinary tract infections. I remember being in ICU following my accident, and telling my nurse I felt as if I was coming down with the flu. She tested my urine immediately, and it showed I had an infection. I had experienced UTI's prior to getting injured, and they were bad enough then. Getting one after a spinal cord injury is horrible. You feel like you have the worst flu ever.

People with spinal cord injuries are prone to UTI's. I experienced them for almost twenty years. I've dealt with IV antibiotics at home, weeks of painful injections and dozens of hospital visits. The worst thing was, I felt chronically lousy. There is a difference between being sick and being injured, and I give so much credit to folks dealing with a condition that makes them feel ill the majority of the time.

Almost a year ago, my infectious disease doctor shared some new research with me. He said that people suffering from UTI's, injured or not, should forego antibiotics and instead, flush their bladder with an insane amount of fluids. Research had proved this more effective, as bacterias have become resistant to antibiotics from society's overuse of them.

So I started drinking. Vodka, gin… Any clear liquid I could get my hands on. That's what my doctor had recommended… Clear liquids. No, just kidding. But it would be fun if that's what was needed, wouldn't it? I drank water, and a lot of it. I had a very severe UTI when I began my water fall, but I was determined not to go the antibiotic route. By the third day, I was up to one gallon of water per day, and I started to feel its positive effects. By the fifth day, my infection was gone.

This was a huge accomplishment for me. Not only did I get rid of the current infection I had, I knew I could prevent new infections from occurring, simply by drinking water. Drinking the amount of water I currently do not only eradicated UTI's, but also helps my skin stay in great shape and my digestive system functions better. I think the best part is I no longer live in fear of having a UTI occur and the suffering and frustration that goes along with them.

5. Skin Issues. Our skin is our biggest organ. As with any organ, some things keep it healthy and other things break it down. If you are an individual who uses a wheelchair full-time, the skin on your tush takes a beating from the constant pressure of sitting. Skin needs circulation to stay healthy, and when there is pressure on it, the circulation is compromised.

Infections from skin breakdown is the number one complication that will take the life of a person with a spinal cord injury. The great thing is, skin breakdown is 100% preventable. The bad thing is, once it gets started, it's a runaway train traveling at warp speed faster then you can imagine. Faster than even I can imagine, and I've experienced its horrors many times.

Skin breakdown happens from the inside out. This is where the danger lies. By the time something significant presents itself on the outside, you are dealing with part of your body missing on the inside. To heal this awful truth requires months of IV antibiotics, months in the hospital having multiple surgeries followed by months of bed rest at home. If pressure is applied to the newly healed area, everything will fall apart. If you are wheelchair-bound, you cannot stand, so your only other choice is to lie in bed.

With all of these challenges, prevention is key. Do your best to prevent getting cold. Do your best to prevent getting hot. Have a backup plan in place if an aide does not come to work. Do your best to prevent UTI's and skin breakdown. Don't worry about asking people for what you need to accomplish these things. The worst they can do is say no. If you suffer from a complication, you are the one paying the highest price.

Keep reading for the "The Top Five List Of The Most Fabulous Things About Living With A Spinal Cord Injury."

Technology, Disabilities and Fun

Some individuals are born with disabilities and others become disabled throughout their lifetime due to injury or disease. Some disabilities happen quickly and others take time to progress. Regardless of when you become disabled or how you become disabled, you are going to do things differently than a person who doesn't have a disability.

Technology makes things easier, more convenient and more fun for people without disabilities. For people with disabilities, it makes things possible. I am writing this using computerized voice activated technology, a.k.a. Siri. Without Siri, (or something like her), a person who does not have enough hand function to type would have a tough time using a keyboard.

Ten years ago, I wrote a book. It was a memoir, consisting of a hundred and twenty pages and it took me an entire year to write it. Not because it required an extensive amount of research, not because I went through months of writer's block. I wrote almost every single day, but the voice activated technology was so poor, I could type faster by using a "typing peg."

A typing peg acts as one plastic finger strapped to your hand and your arm does the work. Since, at the time, my right arm wasn't strong enough to type, I wrote my entire book using one finger. If my way of typing was faster than the best voice activated software available at the time, you can imagine how well the software worked.

Today, I am able to write as fast as if I could type about forty words a minute, including corrections, because of the advances in voice technology. I can also dial my phone, use my computer and my television through the magic of voice technology. And now there is the Google Glass.

Google glass is a wearable, non intrusive gadget that doesn't get in the way of daily life. It's a stylish pair of glasses packed with Bluetooth, Wi-Fi, GPS, speakers, a camera, microphone, touchpad, and a gyroscope that detects head tilts. Sounds fun for anybody, right?! But imagine for a moment what this could do for someone who is paralyzed??!! (Can you tell I'm getting excited...)

Life pauses for no one. My disability involves paralysis. When the moment moves me, I cannot grab my cell phone and snap a picture of a moment I want to remember. I have to have somebody do it for me, and many times, the moment is lost. With Google Glass, all I have to do is say "take a photo," and my memory is captured. I would no longer miss out on the faces and places I want to obtain in a picture.

Video works much the same. I'll be using Google Hangout for group conferences in my new business, and I could do them right from Google Glass. I could also dictate text messages, text videos and pictures, never get lost again and learn about my surroundings (in real time if I chose) when I travel. Google Glass simply requires a Wi-Fi or mobile connection to activate its features, and works with both Android phones and iPhones.

The first Google Glass prototype weighed over eight pounds. Now, its new style choices are feather light and receive nods from the fashion industry. Pretty and practical is my favorite fabulous combination.

The technological world has developed countless products that would not only make more things possible for a person with a disability to experience, but also make more things FUN. I feel society forgets at times people with disabilities just wanna have fun, too... Regardless of the challenges they may experience. All the more reason to, actually.

While I consider myself pretty mobile, my power chair does have its limits; it's only made to travel on flat surfaces. Enter the Action Trackchair. It can go through snow, mud and wooded areas. How fabulous it would be to have my Google Glass on, using my Trackchair, as I went cavorting around my five acres (or anywhere else I desired that wasn't flat), taking pictures as I wished, maybe looking up a certain type of tree I didn't recognize. Sounds like Heaven.

There is one problem. In the world of disabilities, Heaven cost money. Any item with a disability label on it has a huge price tag, and most folks with disabilities I know are spending their money on urological supplies, home health aides, prescriptions and medical bills.

There are so many nonprofit organizations offering amazing, generous support for people with disabilities who need financial assistance. There should be a "Fun Foundation" or something of the sort, with its sole mission being assisting disabled individuals in getting recreational "gadgets", both big and small, so they can experience fun when ever they wish.

Nobody's life, disabled or able bodied, should just consist of the daily necessities. You deserve to have some fun.

Drastic Situations Call For Drastic Measures

Sometimes in life, drastic situations call for drastic measures. For instance... Your babysitter calls in sick on a day when you have a presentation at work. Another company has flown in specifically for it and there is a huge promotion on the line if you're able to sell your company's idea. What do you do?

If you've seen the film, "One Fine Day," you know Michelle Phieffer's character is a single mom dealing with that exact situation. Calling everyone she can think of to watch her little boy and having absolutely no luck, she brings him to work and takes drastic measures to hide him from her boss. Amidst Hollywood hijinks, she's able to make her presentation and it's a huge success. It's a very fine day indeed.

I know it's Hollywood, but we've all been in situations where there is a lot riding on our performance or a set of circumstances, and the cost of failure will come at a high price. We are out of resources, because if we had any, we'd be using them, so we need to think of something unique. And effective. And quickly.

Drastic measures usually come into play when we need a different resource, we need it to be a sure thing and we need it now. I have been in quite a few of these situations, especially after my injury. I'm the one that has labeled them "drastic", but I'll share one with you and see what you think.

About twelve years ago, I moved from L.A. back to Pine Bush. I was planning on living with my dad, in an upstairs apartment in his house. The state had a program I qualified for that helped individuals with disabilities integrate back into the workforce. They modified my van for me so I would have reliable transportation and were going to put an elevator in my home, as my home would also serve as an office.

The elevator was a pretty big project. We were at the stage of the contractor cutting a huge hole in the side of my house where the opening of the elevator would be on the second floor. It just so happened we were going to have heavy rain over the next few days and it was important my contractor finish the area he was working on so we wouldn't have any major leaks.

He showed up in the morning, needing to talk to me. He said he was due a large payment from the state but had not yet received it. When he called, they said a mistake had been made and he would not receive his money for another six weeks. He was very nice, but he explained he could not continue to work on my job without getting paid when he thought he would. He was a small, one man band and had a family to feed.

He said he would be back as soon as the payment came in and would have to work on another job until then. I asked him if I got his money tomorrow, would he come the following day? With a raised eyebrow, he said yes.

I spent the rest of the day researching who exactly was responsible for this mistake. That's the person I wanted to see. Once I found out, I made my plan. I called the aide that was working with me the following day to let her know what my plans were, and she was very supportive. I also called my lawyer. When I told him what I was going to do, he thought I was crazy but said call him if need be.

There were two people I needed to meet with. One was the woman who lost my contractor's voucher, made a new one and put it at the bottom of the pile to be paid. The next person was her boss. I was hoping I could explain my situation, get a check cut and leave.

I arrived at their offices at 7 am. The receptionist was there but the two people I need to meet with not due in until 8 o'clock. I wouldn't explain why I was there, I just said I had an emergency and needed to speak with both of them. I had their names from my research.

The woman was the first to arrive and after a brief explanation from me, she said there was nothing she could do about the situation and my contractor would have to wait. "These things happen," she said. "There's nothing I can do. Bruce "Smith" is my boss and he's who you need to talk to." She went into her office, picked up the phone and shut the door. What a nice, empathetic, buck passing broad.

About fifteen minutes later, Bruce arrived. I could tell by the way he looked at me, he knew who I was and why I was there. He invited me into his office with a smile and shut the door. I explained my situation. He agreed it was unfortunate and his office was responsible for the mistake, but there was nothing he could do about it. Checks were not written in his office, they came from a location in Albany and were part of a bureaucratic process.

I planted my wheelchair right next to his desk, facing him and close enough so I could rest my left arm on it. I told him I had rain coming in a huge hole in my house. I told him I needed an installment of $7000.00 so my contractor would come to work the next day. I told him I was going to sit right where I was until I had a check for that amount in my hand and I did not care where it came from... Albany, Pluto or his very own bank account.

By noon, he was getting annoyed. I had not moved an inch and he said if it came time to close the building and I was still there, he would have no choice but to call the police to have me escorted out or arrested. I said I had a few newspapers waiting to hear from me and if he wanted pictures of me in handcuffs, being forced out of his building as I told my story, go right ahead and call the authorities. I still wasn't moving.

The newspaper story was a bluff on my part, but it worked. Bruce started making phone calls and by 4:30 pm that afternoon, he had arranged for a courier from Albany to bring a check in the amount of

$7000.00 to my home that evening. I reiterated to him I would not leave his office without check in hand, so he might want to reroute his courier.

Around 8 PM, the courier showed up at Bruce's office with my check. Upon my request, my aide had called a few of my friends throughout the day, so I had some support waiting for me in the parking lot. Bruce said not a word to me as we left, just got in his car and turned the key. That was fine by me... I had to stare at the guy all day long. I had my fill of him, too.

I was physically and emotionally drained. I had sat in one position for over twelve hours without a bathroom break and only a few sips of water. To be fair, Bruce offered me some of his lunch, as I watched him eat it at his desk six inches away from me, but I would have rather starved.

I called my contractor when I got home, told him I had his payment and he said he'd see me tomorrow. By the end of the week, he also received the entire amount to complete the project, even though it was far from completion. I guess they weren't taking any chances on the possibility of having to see me again.

It's unbelievable the drastic measures we must take at times to get what we need and what we have been promised. My heart goes out to those who don't have the physical or mental capability to stand up for themselves and fight for what they are entitled to.

Chapter 3:
THE BUREAUCRACY OF HEALTHCARE

SOS!

In today's economy, it's difficult finding employment. I am chronically short staffed in my home, always needing home health aides. Ironically, the most jobs created nationwide over the last twelve months have been for home health aides.

So with me needing staff, and with a multitude of folks becoming home health aides, it would make sense I would have a large response of people looking for work when I advertise for care. Not so.

90% of the individuals who respond to my classified advertisements are individuals you would not allow on your property, let alone in your home. This is true regardless if I'm advertising through newspapers, craigslist, Hudson Valley Help Wanted or word of mouth.

Why is this? Why is good help so hard to find? I used to think it was due to the job's rate of pay. You are not going to get rich being a home health aid, so I've increased salaries out of my own pocket to pay more than my benefit's allow.

I've paid health insurance premiums. I've had monthly bonus programs, rewarding people for not missing a day of work in one month. I've allowed aides to come in late, leave early, and still pay them for a full shift.

I've hired a cleaning person, as to make less work for my aides. I've hired drivers to take me to appointments for the same reason; to make less work for my aides. All of these extras come out of my pocket, but if it improved my staff situation, it would be worth every penny.

I've considered I'm a horrible person to work for. I'm a total care individual, and I cannot change it. I refuse to spend my life in bed so nobody has to be bothered with the routine of helping me get up. If that was my choice, why bother existing?

I've spoken with many individuals who require home health care for themselves or for a family member. I've gone on forums to read other people's experiences and to share mine. I told myself before I did this research, if nobody else had difficulties finding and keeping good staff, I would have to do some soul-searching and see what my problem was.

The nightmare was not my own. Every single person I read about or spoke with shared the same problems I did. Regardless of pay increases, less responsibility for same pay, incentives, perks and bonuses, good help in the home healthcare industry was a rarity.

Once when I was placing a classified advertisement in our local newspaper, the person on the other end of the phone gave me her sympathy. When I started explaining life is good regardless of my disability, blah blah blah, she stopped me in my tracks.

She said the reason she felt bad was because ill intending individuals preyed upon ads like mine. I was shocked. And she was shocked I was shocked, especially after I told her I had been dealing with the same circumstances for years.

From what I've gathered, it is very easy to get "qualified" by a home health care agency to become an aide. It is also a job program the state will pay for if you are unemployed or are at certain income level.

If you are choosing to take care of another human being, there is only one reason you should do it. Because you want to. Not because you feel obligated, not because the training for it was easy to get and paid for by somebody other than yourself, and not because you think it may be the easiest of the jobs available.

I feel as if I should say something along the lines of, "And *certainly* not if you have ill intentions and are taking the job to take advantage of the individual you will be caring for."

Yes, you would think that's an obvious one. But you have a conscience. In addition, a friend of mine who is writer gave me the advice of never asking my readers to, "Read between the lines." So there it is, in black and white.

I have had things stolen from me right out of my wallet, my home, my car and my bank accounts by former aides while they were at work, with me in the next room. And when they are caught red handed, whether by me or a security camera, they could give two shits.

The only ones who care are the ones who have done something bad enough they are facing jail time. My life is challenging as it is, as all of ours are. I do not appreciate individuals who go out of their way to make it more so.

If I catch someone committing a crime against me, it's over... The damage is done. You can bet, however, I follow through with the law for two reasons. One, the individual needs to know they can't do wrong to their fellow human beings and get away with it.

Second, I do not want this person to ever be able to take care of someone else they could possibly do the same thing to. I think of folks who may not have the ability to speak up for themselves... children, the elderly, the mentally, developmentally and emotionally disabled. Can you imagine what kind of damage an ill intending person could do to them?

Although good help is hard to find, there are some true gems out there, and I have had the privilege of working with them. Some aides use my job as a stepping stone towards nursing school or physical therapy school. They are fantastic when they are here, and that's what counts.

It's my pleasure to give them good references forever... They deserve it. Some pick being a home health aide as a career. Bottom line...There is nothing I appreciate more than a good aide. They help my life stay productive and organized, my body healthy and my spirit happy.

Is it Really That Hard To Be Honest?

Over the holidays, I ran a classified ad for help wanted for personal care aides. We usually get quite a large response... somewhere in the neighborhood of two hundred phone calls. Ironically, many times not one applicant is appropriate for the job. I have better odds in Vegas.

I've had other people manage my classified advertisement responses for me. Perhaps I was doing something wrong. I've been hiring people for twenty years. Maybe I sounded burnt out and unenthusiastic during the phone screening and interview process. But everyone else who tries has the same experience.

People make interview appointments and pull no-calls, no-shows. They lie on their resumes. They lie about their work related experience. They make up references. They say they have clean backgrounds when they don't.

Case and point. I interviewed a girl named Tiffany* a few weeks ago from my latest classified ad. She was nineteen years old and very enthusiastic. During the interview, I explained in detail what the position entailed. I also said we do a DMV and background check. I make it a point to tell each interviewee, even if you had a charge as a minor that is a sealed record, I will be made aware of it.

In the DMV check, if someone has a DWI or their license revoked in the last ten years, I cannot hire them. I also explained the details of the background check we would do on her. I said what I always say in interviews... if there is something in your background, you should tell me now and save us both a lot of time because in the end, I will find out.

Tiffany triple reassured me her background and license were perfectly clean. I gave her the necessary paperwork that needed to be completed for the position. I also explained the physical requirements. She asked me if once her physical requirements were completed, was the job hers?

I told Tiffany becoming an employee in my home was a process. First, an interview. If the interview goes well, the next step is getting your physical requirements completed. I explained the physical requirements needed to be 100% complete before anyone can be on the books to get paid.

Next, there is training involved. First, I show potential aides how to transfer (move) me from my wheelchair into bed and then vice versa. They have to be successful in this area before we move on to additional training. Simply put, needing to be transferred is one of the main reasons I need home care.

After successful transfer training, we move on to morning training. The trainee aide shadows one of my aides as I get up, showered and ready for the day. The trainee is shown around my home to know where things are, and also shown how my wheelchair accessible van works.

I told Tiffany if her physical requirements, her transfer training and her hands on training were all successfully completed, the job was hers. Keeping the job was another matter.

She had to be dependable, on time and remain trustworthy. I told her dependability and trustworthy were the only two things I could not teach her. I also explained she had to continue to meet my needs in order to keep her job.

She was super excited. After our interview, she said she was going to call her doctor's office and set up an appointment immediately. Since everybody's financial circumstances are different, I recommended her to the health center in our town. They charged on a sliding scale, the clinic was clean and they accepted walk-ins every day.

My first red light regarding Tiffany should have been how long it took her to complete her physical requirements. While it normally takes a new aide about a week to get everything done, it took her over three.

After a lot of attempts, she was successful in transfer training and she completed the hands-on training. I helped her fill out the remaining paperwork and sent everything to my insurance company to await approval.

Usually it takes about seventy-two hours for the results of a background and DMV check to be completed. In the meantime, Tiffany started working. It's entirely reasonable for people to be nervous starting a new job and not remember everything they learned in training. With Tiffany, it was as if she was never received any training at all.

She could not transfer me, even after being retrained again and again. She would not use Universal Precautions, i.e. gloves, regardless how much I reminded her. I would make a list of chores for her to do while she was at work, and they would fail to get done, even though she would say she had completed them when I asked her. She was too scared to drive me anywhere. Bottom line, she could not meet my needs.

Her background check came back soiled. *Very soiled.* Part of me wasn't surprised because the results were taking much longer to come back than usual. When I asked her about it, she said she was charged as a minor and it was a sealed record. I reminded her of our interview conversation and also pointed out the documents she signed, stating the information she gave was the truth, upon penalty of perjury.

I was mad. Being short staffed is extremely stressful. I had just wasted a month waiting for this girl to start working with me. When I told her she could not be an employee of mine and why, she was shocked. She said she was entitled to her position here, due to all the hard work she put in to get the job.

When people start arguing with me in these circumstances and I am alone with them, I simply asked them to leave or I will call 911. I don't want to sound dramatic, but people can be very vindictive. I've learned my lesson the hard way.

Tiffany left. I do not think I will be bothered by her again. But I will been running another classified advertisement, looking for staff. Tiffany was not the first of her kind to grace us with her presence. What I'd like to know, is it really that hard to be honest?

Can You Save Me A Seat

About six years ago, I started suffering from significant chest pain and shortness of breath. My pulmonary doctor did a myriad of tests but found nothing significant. My symptoms steadily got worse.

Next, I went to a physiatrist who specialized in people with spinal cord injuries. She assured me my symptoms were very common for people living with SCI. She explained how over time, the back support on my wheelchair tightened and shortened my chest muscles.

The pain I was experiencing were actually muscle spasms. It had become excruciating from sitting in my wheelchair for fourteen years, fourteen hours a day. I had a chronic charley horse in my chest.

It felt like a heart attack. The solution, however, was simple. A new back on my wheelchair would put my upper body in a position to keep my chest stretched out.

When the physiatrist handed me the contact information for the nearest seating clinic, I inwardly cringed. It was at a rehabilitation hospital in West Haverstraw, N.Y. I had a *horrific* experience in their outpatient department the year I was injured.

I was desperate for relief. I took a deep breath and called. And called and called and *called.* I left voice mail messages, I spoke with a secretary I got to know quite well, I even had my doctor call.

If you look in the dictionary under "squeaky wheel", you'll now see my picture. There was a coordinator I needed to speak with before anything could move forward, and it took her a little more then three months to call me back.

Three months. With me leaving *at least* three messages each week. Unbelievable. By now it's December, and my appointment is made for mid-January.

The day of the appointment, I had a sick feeling in my gut. I ended up running a little late... About ten minutes. I called the clinic to let them know. The woman who answered assured me it wasn't a problem and would make sure the appropriate person received my message.

I was exactly twelve minutes late as I breathlessly rushed through the suite doors of the clinic. At the registration desk, I smiled and gave my name to the sour looking woman behind it.

She responded by screaming at me. Yes, *screaming* at me. I was late and had thrown off her schedule. I tried to explain my ninety minute commute, I had called, we couldn't get assistance finding the clinic; anything I could think of for some empathy.

None of it mattered. People were starting to poke their head in the office we were in to see what all the fuss was about. This woman sounded possessed.

I had never been screamed at like this in my life. I turned away so the woman couldn't see the tears hot in my eyes. By this time I was very frustrated and *extremely* out of breath.

It didn't help when the physical therapist I'd be working with introduced himself in an exasperated tone. He couldn't even be bothered to make eye contact with me. He just said in a clipped voice, "Follow me."

My aide and I were practically forced to jog in an attempt to keep up with him. I suddenly stopped in my tracks. I was completely out of breath and still fighting back tears.

I was feeling hopeless about how this rehabilitation hospital could help me. I had waited over three months for this appointment. It didn't matter. My aide, being equally appalled at the experience, helped me find the exit. I got into my car and went home.

I still needed a new wheelchair back. I went to another top rated rehabilitation hospital, this time in White Plains, N.Y. While the people there were noticeably nicer, they didn't work on my brand of chair.

Of course, they didn't tell me this over the phone when I made the appointment. I waited over six weeks to get in, driving almost two hours to get there.

By that time, my chest and I needed relief. I found a home health equipment company in Long Island that was a dealer of the particular back cushion I needed. I placed my order and paid the $800.00 bill. Two weeks later, I had my cushion.

Did I mention both hospitals I went to are on the National Institutes of Health's list of Top Ten Best Rehabilitation Hospital's in the country?

Desperately Seeking Survival Guide

Information. Information is the most valuable commodity in existence. Without it, you cannot make an informed decision. Lives can even be lost if an individual does not have the information they need at the time they need it.

Information is one of the most critical things an individual and their family coping with a catastrophic health crisis needs. Being hit with a health crisis thrusts you and your loved ones into a thick jungle in a foreign country without a map.

Your head is spinning with the who, what, when, where, why and how of your new country. Big problem...you don't speak the language and your life depends on finding a translator.

The extreme stress of finding correct, up to date, critical information in the midst of a catastrophic health crisis should not even be a factor. The patient and their family should have the "luxury" of putting all their energy into the patient getting well and everyone coping with the emotional element of the crisis.

You've been brought to the hospital due to a car accident. Your doctors realize they are dealing with a catastrophic, life altering, permanent health condition. Immediately, an individual who's title is "Survival Guide," should be made to find you and your family.

This person will play an integral role in your healthcare team until the day you leave the hospital. Initially, they will explain what their job is…To ensure you and your family's needs are met during your hospital stay. A catastrophic health crisis is a family health crisis. It affects everyone, so everyone will have their own needs.

First. Your doctors. Your Survival Guide should be sure you have the best doctors available for your specific conditions. If you or a family member want a second, third or tenth opinion, your Survival Guide should be supportive and assist in arranging them.

Next. To negotiate with your private insurance company to squeeze the most out of every dollar your policy entitles you to. In catastrophic health situations, insurance companies do a lot of bargaining because bottom line, you are giving them a large amount of guaranteed business.

This is an extremely important part of your process. It should be done by a person use to dealing with insurance companies… Not by someone who is inexperienced and overwrought with stress and grief.

Next. You should be made aware of every government and nonprofit organization in existence. Your Survival Guide should help you apply to any of these organizations that could possibly benefit you.

It is imperative any applications be processed as soon as possible. Many of these agencies give out a certain amount of financial assistance annually. Once the amount is met, they do not give out any more until the following year.

Next. As stated earlier, catastrophic injuries affect your entire family. Your Survival Guide should make counseling available immediately for everyone involved. Then the Survival Guide should take a step back and allow people to grieve as they will.

At the time I was initially injured, one counselor told me I had a severe problem because, according to her, I was not experiencing the stages of grief in the proper order. I had two things to say about that...

Everyone experiences grief differently, not right or wrong... that much I knew. Next, I asked my dad to open my hospital room door so she could leave. I was lucky to never see her and her ugly clipboard again.

There are dozens of questions on how something like this could come into fruition. Would it be a government funded program, would it be based hospital by hospital, you would need a team of people in each facility because of the amount of work involved... It would be quite a project to facilitate, but if a man can be put on the moon, a program such as I described can come into fruition.

I know one thing for sure. Something like this is desperately needed. I only mentioned a few things. There are more... Many more. My family and I lived it. We were in a country where we didn't speak the language and did not have a map, tour guide, or even a compass. It made my injury all the more terrifying.

Billions of dollars are spent each year on health care in this country. How to make this a priority to Washington? To the insurance companies? I don't know. Perhaps they would have to experience it for themselves.

Standing Up To The Lions Of Injustice

I have met dozens of amazing individuals throughout my journey of living with a spinal cord injury. In the summer of 2008, I was introduced to someone unlike any other I had met to date.

Eddie Ryan was a Marine who was wounded in Iraq in 2005. When I met him, he was twenty-four years old. I had met his dad, Chris Ryan, the year before at my foundation's annual golf outing fundraiser.

Every year at our foundation's annual golf outing, we make donations to individuals living with disabilities, or organizations who assist people living with disabilities. That year, one of our donations went to Eddie Ryan.

Eddie had been unable to attend the outing with his dad. Chris Ryan was a really lovely person and it was a pleasure meeting him. I had also spoken with Eddie's mom over the phone after the outing. I promised them I would visit Eddie in the very near future.

I'm embarrassed to say although the Ryan's only lived about twenty minutes away from me, it took me a few months to visit Eddie. The Ryan's lived in a beautiful area of Ellenville, but I teased Angie you needed an Army tank to make it up their mountain of a driveway.

The first thing you notice about Eddie when you met him is his *size*. His biceps are as big as my thighs and his thighs are as big as my waist. He is *not* someone I would want to make enemies with.

Eddie uses a wheelchair full-time due to a traumatic brain injury sustained in Iraq. Eddie was hit with two bullets in his frontal lobe from friendly fire. His positive spirit and attitude are palpable the instant you set eyes on him.

His parents were fighting desperately to get their son the care he needed; physical, occupational and speech therapy, and the ever elusive home health care. The Ryan's were being told by the government due to the rural area they lived in, the services Eddie needed were nearly impossible to provide.

The government was, however, doing its best to convince the Ryan's their son would be better off in a Veterans Long Term Care Facility. How can this possibly be?!

Eddie Ryan sacrificed part of his body and his mind to ensure a blanket of freedom and democracy for his county. Now, his country is passing the buck simply because they are finding Eddie's and thousands of other vets needs *difficult* to meet?

Did Eddie pass the buck when the opportunity arose? No. Eddie *volunteered* to stand up against the lions of injustice for us and now it is our duty to stand up to the injustice being done to Eddie and those like him.

The thousands of wounded vets who came to their country's aide now needs aide from their country. How can you help? Write your congressman or local representative, find out about wounded vets living in your area and volunteer to assist in their daily needs, organize a fundraiser or an awareness rally or write an editorial for your local newspaper.

Society should be doing anything and everything to raise awareness of this tragic injustice. As all improvements in society, this begins in our own backyards. The men and women of the American Armed Forces are armed and ready when we need them. It should work both ways.

A Few Cracks In Home Health Care

If you are an individual with a disability, living at home and require help with your personal care needs, (bathing, dressing, etc.), then you need to hire home health aides. When I was initially injured and going through my first hiring process, I was extremely naïve. I thought all home health aides would be a version of Florence Nightingale.

Unfortunately, for anyone needing home health aides, it is far from true. In my experience, for every one wonderful individual that has nothing but the best of intentions, there are twenty that prey upon individuals like myself, looking only to take advantage. Other folks I talk to in my same situation have the same experiences. To this day, I do not know why this is.

I moved to Los Angeles the second year after my injury. There was a clinic doing groundbreaking physical therapy for people with spinal cord injuries, and I wanted to see what it was all about. Almost immediately upon my arrival, I met a woman at the physical therapy clinic who ran a home health agency.

As when anybody moves, you need to set up house…call the electric company, the cable company and if you're me, you also call your local home health care agency. Hiring people to care for you in your home is a big job, so when a woman who runs a home health care agency practically fell into my lap at my physical therapy clinic, I thought it too good to be true. Turned out, it was.

The woman's name was Sheridan, and she said she had the perfect live-in aide for me. The aide, whose name was Winnie, had taken care of Sheridan's mother for five years. "She is salt of the earth. I would trust her with my own life," Sheridan said.

A few days after Winnie moved in, I sent her to do some errands for me. She used my van, as she did not have her own car. She should have been gone a few hours, two at the most, and she left about 3 PM. By 7 PM, with no sign of Winnie or my van, I called Sheridan's twenty-four hour emergency line.

By 10 PM, there was still no sign of my aide, my van or a return phone call from the dozen messages I left on Sheridan's voicemail. I had called a few friends earlier to come over and help me figure out what to do. We called local hospitals to see if anybody fitting Winnie's description had been recently admitted to any emergency rooms, but no luck. We also called the police to report my van stolen.

Close to midnight, I received a phone call from a very lively sounding gentleman who introduced himself as JJ. He said Winnie had been arrested, my van was impounded but it was "A-OK!" As I started to ask questions, he hung up.

With the help of my friends, by the following morning I had my van back safe and sound and was aware of the facts from the police. Winnie had driven my van to downtown L.A., and tried to sell the TV,

VCR and Nintendo in it for some quick cash to buy crack. I had a Ford Mark III Conversion Van at the time that comes with all the extras you end up never using.

When Winnie's potential customer was not interested in television appliances, she offered him oral sex instead. He wasn't interested in that either… He was an undercover cop. Winnie was arrested and my van was impounded, just as JJ said.

A friend had stayed overnight to help me the following day. I had never heard from Sheridan and by then, never expected to. My van was back safe and sound, and I considered myself lucky to be rid of Sheridan's services if Winnie was an example of the caliber of individuals she had in her agency.

The police told me Winnie had quite an arrest record for a resume, so obviously no background check had been done on her prior to Sheridan placing her in my home. (Sheridan had assured me she did extensive background checks on all of her aides.) Even more disturbing, the police were familiar with Sheridan herself. Apparently, she spent time outside the Los Angeles County Jail, telling individuals who were being released she could offer them a job that would provide them with a roof over their head and the use of a vehicle.

Around noon that day, I had a knock on my door. When my friend opened it, I couldn't believe my eyes. Winnie was standing there, suitcase in hand, expecting to return to work. When I told her to leave before I called the police, she claimed Sheridan told her to go back to work as soon as she was able. As my friend picked up the phone to call 911, Winnie fled. I never saw or heard from her again.

Later that afternoon, I got a call from Sheridan. She was furious I had told Winnie to leave, and said I was not honoring my part of the contract I signed with her agency. I asked her if she knew of Winnie's actions the prior day, and she accused me of being prejudice against people with addictions.

"Addiction is a disease!" Sheridan exclaimed. I told her I fully agreed. I also told her a person dealing with drug addiction had no business taking care of another individual when they needed care themselves. I hung up the phone while she was still ranting. I never heard from or saw her again, either.

Going through that experience was traumatic, especially being three thousand miles away from home. But now, anytime I tell it, I am filled with laughter. It's also fun to watch people's reaction as I tell it. These kinds of stories can't be made up. That's because truth is usually stranger than fiction.

The ABC's of Healthcare

I go to a doctor for one reason, and one reason only; their expertise.

After living with a spinal cord injury for twenty years, I have gotten to know my body extremely well, and when something is awry I can tell if is serious enough where I need to see a doctor or if it is an issue I can handle from home.

Recently, I had a headache accompanied with zero appetite and nausea that stayed with me all day. Since I am not a person who deals with headaches on a regular basis, I was paying particular attention to my symptoms from their onset.

Of course this had to happen on a Friday, as most inconvenient things do, and we were having a few family and friends over for cocktails and laughs. My headache literally started five minutes after I finalized our evening plans, and as it escalated throughout the day, I figured I would just sip water instead of wine and blame the fact I didn't want to partake in dinner on a big, late lunch.

About fifteen minutes after our guests left that evening, I dialed 911. My headache had suddenly worsened and I could feel my blood pressure climbing rapidly.

Something important to note about people living with spinal cord injuries... A condition called "autonomic dysreflexia" comes into play that can raise an individual's blood pressure high enough to cause a stroke. Simply put, it's my body's way of "automatically" telling me something is significant wrong.

The good thing about this condition is my blood pressure will magically go back to normal the moment the problem causing the dysreflexia is alleviated. The bad thing about this condition is my blood pressure will continue to rise until the problem causing the dysreflexia is alleviated.

My normal blood pressure is 90/60 and by the time I got to the emergency room, it was 197/104… needless to say, I was scared. In the emergency room, we checked every part of my body to find an infection or some other explanation as to why I was so dysreflexic.

In my own mind, I was thinking along the lines of "what came first, the chicken or the egg? " Did I have a terrible headache that made me dysreflexic or was I dysreflexic for another reason? (Autonomic dysreflexia comes with a headache because of the elevated blood pressure.)

Finding nothing in the ER, I was admitted for observation and was scheduled to see a neurologist the following day. It was 6:30 a.m. by the time I finally got in an actual hospital room… I had been in the ER for over nine hours. My headache was no better than when I had first arrived at the ER, my blood pressure was jumping all over the place and all I wanted to do was talk to the neurologist to get a plan of care started to find out what the hell was wrong with me.

When a doctor finally came in my room, claiming himself as the neurologist, I nearly wept with relief. He was very nice but had a heavy Russian accent, and I left the hospital still not knowing his name.

As he examined me and asked me questions about my medical history, I asked him how we control the dysreflexia until we find out what is wrong. When he asked me to repeat myself, I simply assumed he hadn't heard me, but that was not the case. He had no idea what autonomic dysreflexia was.

I stared at him in horror. I could not believe this was the individual whose hands my life was in. I explained again, hoping it was something to do with a language barrier. It was not. He thanked me for teaching him something new and I asked to see his boss. He informed me because it was a weekend, he was the only neurologist available.

After forty eight hours of Dr. Russia treating me for a severe migraine, receiving fluids and heavy doses of pain medicine, my headache and blood pressure finally eased. When I returned home and was able to make sleep part of the equation, I felt even better.

It remains to be seen if I am now a migraine sufferer or if what I experienced was just a fluke. Dr. Russia had no idea when I asked him. I am confident the neurologist I have seen in the past at Columbia-Presbyterian in New York City, who knows what autonomic dysreflexia is, will have some answers.

Until I see my neurologist at Columbia, I feel somewhat like a ticking time bomb. What do I do if I get another headache accompanied with dysreflexia? How do I bring my blood pressure down so I do not have a stroke until I am able to get professional help? And what professional help is available to me… a hospital twenty minutes away where the neurologists don't even know the definition of the life-threatening condition I suffer from, let alone how to treat it?!

Autonomic dysreflexia may sound complicated to the laymen, but it is ABC for neurologists Universally. Our country is in a great debate regarding health care. The fact there are laws regarding it apparently mean nothing. One aspect I believe each wing would agree on is health care is expensive and there is a significant amount of waste in it.

If waste was eliminated, care would improve and insurance premiums would go down. I have yet to see the bill for my recent hospital visit, but after nine hours in the ER, two CAT scans, multiple x-rays, bloodwork, dozens of medications, a one to one aide in my hospital room with me around-the-clock because I cannot use a call bell due to my paralysis, topped off with a neurology consult and being an inpatient for a total of forty-eight hours, I am easily looking at a bill in the high tens of thousands.

A portion of the payment of this bill will come out of my pocket due to recent cuts in Medicare, which is my primary insurance. New York State Medicaid is my secondary insurance, but because their reimbursement rate is so low, not many facilities accept them as payment.

And I still have to go to another neurologist because the one I saw as an inpatient (which was the whole reason I was admitted and not sent home) didn't know his ABC's.

Next time a specialist is presented to me, I'm going to clarify this first by asking him or her to recite their ABC's. As health care consumers, we all have to advocate for ourselves. Might as well cover all the bases and start at the beginning.

The World's Worst Health Insurance...The Veteran's Administration

In a previous article, I introduced you to Eddie Ryan. Eddie was twenty-four years old when I met him in 2008. He is a Marine who sustained a severe traumatic brain injury from friendly fire while serving in Iraq.

Eddie lived with his parents, and the government was encouraging them to place Eddie in a long term care facility. The Ryan's lived in a rural area of Upstate New York. Due to their living location, our government found it just too difficult in getting Eddie the home care he was entitled to.

Hearing this from Eddie's mom, Angie, I asked her if I could post an ad on craigslist to advertise for home health aides and different types of therapists Eddie needed. Angie readily agreed, saying if I found the appropriate individuals, the Veteran's Administration would take care of the rest.

Posting the ad took five minutes and didn't cost a dime. Within a few days, I had five people for Angie to interview. She was quickly able to hire a lovely woman who conveniently lived within ten minutes from the Ryan's home.

When Angie told me of her success, I was thrilled. The woman wanted full-time work, which is exactly what Eddie needed. Finding a new full-time aide that foot's your bill after only a few days of advertising is something to be celebrated!

Angie explained, however, the new aide would only be working part time for her first month of employment. Knowing how desperately the Ryan's needed aide care, I asked Angie why.

The Ryan's had to pay this woman out of their own pocket until the Veterans Administration sent a representative to the Ryan's to meet with the new employee and register them properly. Care is expensive, and the Ryan's could only afford to pay someone for two eight hour shifts a week.

Angie said it would be at least one month before the V.A. could send a representative. According to the V.A., this was due to the Ryan's "out of the way" geographical location and the backlog of veterans who needed to be enrolled for care.

What is wrong with our system of healthcare for the men and women who volunteer to defend our nation? I hear these heart-wrenching stories over and over and over again, and I just don't get it.

Was it "out of the way" for Angie Ryan to travel to a hospital in Germany when her son was at death's door from being shot in the head twice while defending his country? Was it "out of the way" for Chris and Angie Ryan to make arrangements to bring their severely injured son home to live with them instead of sticking him in a long-term care facility?

Who is defending our veterans and ensuring they get the care they need and deserve? Who is speaking for them if they do not have the ability to speak for themselves? Who does the government think is going to provide financial means for our veterans to get health care if they do not?

I think government health care for veterans is the worst workman's compensation insurance I have ever seen. And whatever individual, committee or organization responsible for veteran's care, should be ashamed of themselves.

For it to take a month or more for the V.A. to coordinate a visit to register a home health aide, particularly for a total care individual, is simply unacceptable. This young man and his parents aren't waiting to get his teeth capped.

Eddie has a traumatic brain injury and needs constant, twenty-four hour care. He also needs therapies to help him heal, get strong and stay strong. Without outside help, all of the responsibility of Eddie's care is put on his family.

My own family experienced what Eddie and his parents did. My father was a Korean War vet, and used his V.A. insurance for cancer treatment. His in-patient and out-patient care were disastrous. My dear dad lived with cancer for seven years before it took his life.

There was one surgery in particular where a CAT scan performed post surgery showed a large cancerous area previously tattooed in a colonoscopy was still in my father's body. Tattooing cancerous areas is standard procedure pre-surgery so surgeons can easily see what is needed to be removed during surgery.

This was a huge miss on the surgeon's part. Worse yet, my father had to go back into the O.R. in a very weakened condition from just having surgery. After the second surgery, he never quite got back to the strength he was prior to the first surgery. I believe too much was asked of his body in too short of time.

As a family, our hands were full getting Dad the best care we could. Suing the doctor who made this mistake was something some of us seriously considered. At the time, however, it was just too much for us to pursue. We wanted to put all of our energy and effort into Dad's care. After Dad was gone, a lawsuit seemed pointless.

Eddie and my dad are lucky. Regardless of having horrible health insurance, their families advocate for them and do everything possible to get them the best care. Many other veterans are on their own.

I believe it is society's responsibility to step up and change things for our country's veterans. Drastic situations call for drastic measures. Our veterans stepped up when our country needed them to. It's unimaginable to think where we would be as a nation if they hadn't. Now it's our turn.

A Paralyzed Government

The American people were stuck, by no fault of their own, between a rock and a hard place, or worse yet, a rock and a rock; The House of Representatives and the Senate. These two rocks make up the boulder that is Congress, and Congress had recently decided to squeeze Americans to the brink of hopelessness and desperation by closing the government.

As a result, workers were furloughed, mothers were having trouble feeding their children since the suspension of the WIC program, the Head-Start program for low income preschool children and their families was shut down and the Centers for Disease Control closed its influenza program that tracks the flu and helps people get vaccinated.

As a disabled American who's life was once almost taken by a raging case of the flu, not being able to get a vaccine would put my life in real danger. Congress became paralyzed, and its condition was contagious, spreading throughout the American people like wildfire.

What was so shameful about our government's circumstances is they chose to be paralyzed, but the American people they are paralyzed had no choice.

A single mother didn't choose to lose her WIC benefits, a four-year-old little boy didn't choose for himself and his family to stop being a part of the Head-Start program and it was not my choice to skip getting the flu vaccine. The programs I am mentioning are only a few examples of what folks were being forced to do without because the government chose to shutdown.

Even the multiple death benefits veterans and their families are entitled were revoked and at the very least, modified. What is happening to the content of moral courage of the country these people sacrificed their lives for?

To this American, the most shameful element in the malfunction of our government is Congress chose to be rocks, having no give, no compromise or thought of accommodation of those they represent. I am not normally a cynical person, but I have come to believe since Congress and their families had what they needed throughout this shutdown, Congress was in no hurry.

Under any circumstances, I do not wish harm or ill health to anyone.

However, I also have come to believe if a member of Congress or their loved ones needed a program that was closed in the shutdown, such as a clinical trial that was a last resort to an individual with cancer, egos would have been placed aside and communication would be the order of the day.

If they really wanted to, the members of Congress would have found some wiggle room in their chosen rock formation and begin taking baby steps towards a government whose sign shines bright with the illuminating words "Welcome, Open 24 Hours".

I end with my favorite quote from Gandhi that keeps me on the path in life I wish to lead, and when I stray, even without meaning to, it always brings me back. "It's the action, not the fruit of the action, that's important. You have to do the right thing. It may not be in your power, may not be in your time, that there'll be any fruit. But that doesn't mean you stop doing the right thing. You may never know what results come from your action. But if you do nothing, there will be no result."

The "No Hit" Policy In Washington

When our founding fathers created the Constitution, they were adamant about it containing the "no-hit policy."

The United States of America was their first baby, the first new world they created and like any parent, they had certain ideals they wanted to ensure were carried out by generations to follow. These brave pioneers were wise enough men to know as their country grew and changed long after they were gone, the Constitution would also need to change to meet the needs of its country.

This is the foundation of the genius behind that glorious document; it can be amended as the citizens of the United States see fit. The "no hit policy", however, was something they were sure would forever be practiced.

Wait a minute…Did I say our founding fathers?! The Constitution?! I must be not getting enough sleep. What I meant to say was how I find it so amusing when soon to be first time parents, (I have a particular friend in mind), with the very best of intentions, insist they will instill a "no-hit" policy in their parenting.

They may even do a bit of criticizing of other parents who give their child an occasional swat on the behind when they misbehave. The parents in waiting believe reasoning and explaining to a child what they are doing wrong, along with perhaps taking a privilege away for a temporary amount of time, is the best way for the child to learn the right thing to do and also has the best chance of the child not doing the same bad behavior over again.

I am not a parent, so I absolutely will not give an opinion on this issue, but strictly as an observer, I can 100% honestly say every parent I know who has set a "no-hit" policy while pregnant with their first born amended it sooner than later.

Since the current members of Congress are acting like misbehaved children, I think they should be treated as such. It is clear reasoning and explaining what they are doing wrong is having no effect whatsoever on them correcting their behavior and making better choices, so I think they should be punished.

While swatting Speaker Boehner on his behind is tempting, lets swat him where it will really hurt; take away a few of his privileges. His paycheck, his health insurance and his tanning bed would be a good start, along with apologizing to the American people for his unacceptable behavior during the government's recent shut down.

Parents make children do that, right? Apologize to the friends they have been unfair to and not shared with very well? Since there seems to be so many children of all ages in Congress these days, I feel the same disciplinary actions should be placed on all of them.

Let them live without the "privileges" so many folks were forced to live without and perhaps they would have made different choices. And what about our President? (Whom I voted for twice.) Since children are taught communicating with a teammate you don't see eye to eye with is always a better solution then fighting and name-calling, our President should always be leading by example and banging down a teammate's door to have a conversation, regardless of who he feels is in the wrong.

Isn't that why we voted for him? To be the example for the rest of us to follow, particularly through difficult times when others may have floundered and not possess a clue of what to do to try and make things better?

As a severely disabled individual, I have had to choose surgeons who I trusted enough to put my life in their hands through extremely complicated surgeries. To me, voting for America's President is as important a choice. Our President is the surgeon who keeps America alive through challenging times, and a surgeon is only as good as the team surrounding him.

Fraying At The Edges

I remember the exact moment I found out two planes had hit the World Trade Center on September 11, 2001.

I was getting ready for the day and for some reason I didn't have the TV on as I usually did. I was calling a friend's spa to make an appointment and when the receptionist answered, she sounded extremely distraught.

"Can you believe what's happening in the city? It's as if the world is ending!" Having no idea what she was talking about, I asked her to explain. As soon as she said two commercial airplanes had hit the World Trade Centers and our government was saying it was a terrorist attack, I immediately turned on the television.

The picture appeared just in time for me to see the first building fall. As I stared in horror at what I was witnessing, there was only one person who came to mind; my brother. He was a lieutenant for FDNY and I did not know if he was working that day.

My heart raced as I dialed his number, and I felt instant relief wash over me as I heard his voice answer. We spoke for a moment or two, and when I asked him what he thought about the possibility of the second building coming down, he simply said, "it's not good."

We all know what happened that day. The second building did fall, bringing thousands of innocent people with it and turning them into dust. Our country was no longer exempt from terrorist attacks, and America's physical and emotional landscape changed forever.

In the days following 9/11, a change that touched me deeply was perhaps one of subtlety, or so I viewed it at the time. It was really more of a shift than a change. I live in a small town about 70 miles Northwest of New York City. Overall, it's a very friendly place, one of those small communities where everybody knows everyone else.

There was still, however, your usual human inpatient's. People generally had a rush focused for their own daily agenda. After 9/11, all of that suddenly went away. Things moved slower. People moved slower. It was as if everyone was taking the time to actually enjoy the process of whatever their day consisted of by living in the moment instead of simply rushing to get to the next thing that they would then rush to get to the next thing and so on and so on, until they flopped into bed at night utterly exhausted, only to do it all again the following day.

Folks also started taking the time to be aware of not only their own day to day existence, but their fellow human being's existence and circumstance. Our little town became more about what we could do for others instead of what we could do for ourselves.

In the twelve years since 9/11, the feeling of unity and possessing a heart to heart connection for one another has frayed at the edges and continues to do so at an accelerating rate. Why does it seem only through tragedy we are enabled to open our eyes to the circumstances of another's existence, instead of being interested in agendas only benefit ourselves? It is shamefully disrespectful to forget the lives lost from 9/11 and any other military campaign where Americans have sacrificed their lives and limbs to ensure we go to bed at night tucked in by a blanket of freedom.

Regardless of yearly memorials and pledges of "We will never forget", we forget them every time we treat our fellow human beings with indifference or intolerance.

I wager, however, the families of the fallen heroes need no reminder and never will. It's scary to think we, as individuals, have to experience intimate loss, grief and suffering before we can make treating one another with kindness and empathy the norm instead of the exception.

The Disabilities of The Americans With Disabilities Act

The Americans With Disabilities Act is a joke. Its revision in 2009 is even more of a joke. It's a wide-ranging civil rights law, protecting people with disabilities from discrimination. After spending hours going through it in a vain attempt to understand it, I understand next to nothing. But I am willing to bet on one thing…the committee who created that act did not possess any idea of what a disabled person needs.

"Reasonable accommodations." I read the words reasonable accommodations thousands of times throughout the ADA and I am still unable to understand its meaning. That's probably because in the Americans With Disabilities Act, it doesn't tell you what it means. It simply states over and over and over again individuals with disabilities are entitled to reasonable accommodations in society.

Jobs, public transportation, public and commercial entities… All are mentioned in the ADA as being places and circumstances where "individuals with disabilities should not be excluded." In my experience, it's safe to say I am "excluded" from 90% of the commercial and municipal establishments I visit. I have to be very relentless and demand to be accommodated so I can enjoy and experience what I came to. Sometimes people are happy to try and accommodate you. Sometimes it's the last thing they want to do.

I spent an hour in my car yesterday as My Mike and I waited for takeout from a lovely, elegant restaurant because I could not fit into their establishment. It was street-level, without steps to get in, so that part was fine. But once inside, nothing fit. The tables were too small for a wheelchair, the bathroom was "accessible", but there was not enough room for me to get into it. Bathroom accessibility is always a crapshoot for wheelchairs. All commercial establishments have to do is place two grab bars in their bathroom to be ADA compliant. I'm paralyzed. What will grab bars do for me?

"Reasonable accommodations" in the job market is another joke. At any individual's place of employment, you need to be able to get into the front door and use the bathroom, at the very, very least. Many commercial buildings have ramps with two or three steps at the end of them you need to go up to get inside. If I could walk up steps, would I need a ramp?

Next, there is the environment inside the workplace. Phones you cannot use, desks you cannot fit under and computers you cannot use. How well is any individual going to perform their job if they don't have what they need in their workplace to do it properly?

The ADA states if an individual with a disability needs a certain accommodation outside of the workplace, the workplace is not obligated to accommodate that individual. I wouldn't expect open arms with a wheelchair waiting for me at my job, but some very inexpensive software so my computer is voice activated (which I need at home, as well) and a table as a desk I can fit under is not too much to ask.

The last job I had working out of the home had phones I couldn't use and a bathroom the size of a hall closet. I had to bring my own computer, external mouse and cell phone with me every day so I could do my work. Believe me, I was not comfortable. I couldn't even fit into the break room, so I ate my lunch outside. Luckily, this job was in Southern California, so I was able to eat in a warm environment. When I moved on from that job, I made a promise to myself I would never again work for a company that didn't think I was worth accommodating.

There needs to be a law that is universally accommodating. It should be created by people with all types of disabilities for people with all types of disabilities...Individuals living with blindness, deafness, paralysis and other physical, mental, emotional and developmental challenges that put them in the minority category of needing things a bit different. If our government can put together a group of individuals making it possible for a man to walk on the moon, they should be able to put together a group of individuals that can accomplish this.

Chapter 4:
THE PLAGUE OF DISCRIMINATION
IN SOCIETY

A Doctor's Scam

If you are an individual living with a permanent disability, I'm sure you've been approached by countless of individuals guaranteeing they can "cure" you, or they have something to offer no one else has to significantly help you.

I stay away from the "cure" folks. While I do believe healing takes place through individuals who have a gift from a higher power, enabling them to tap into resources the average human being cannot, many charlatans exist. Out of the people who declare themselves mediums and healers, I think possibly one out of a thousand are truly gifted.

Individuals with severe disabilities or folks dealing with a terminal illness are unfortunate targets for charlatans. People will pay extraordinary amounts of money to someone who says they have a cure nobody else does. I've sadly witnessed it many times.

It's immoral enough if an individual falsely claims they have healing powers. When a doctor, however, not only preys upon the sick and disabled to offer them false healing modalities, but actually manipulates them into signing their insurance benefits over to him, that is pure evil.

I lived in L.A. for five years following my injury. While I was there, I attended a physical therapy clinic called the PEERS program. It was run by a Dr. Burns out of a small brick building in Beverly Hills. The PEERS program swore it enabled all levels of spinal cord injuries to stand and take steps, using ground breaking physical therapy and something called an RGO Brace.

The "groundbreaking" physical therapy was a one physical therapist, overworked and underpaid. There were a few physical therapy assistants who attempted the same exercises the physical therapist did. Only one of the assistants had a bit of physical therapy training... The rest were kids hired from Taco Bell.

Depending on what type of insurance you had determined whom you got to work with. At the time, I had private health insurance, so I worked with the actual physical therapist. Tens of thousands of dollars was paid to the clinic for my treatment. Another $30,000 was spent on equipment, which was never even used on me.

There was an interesting mix of patients at the PEERS program. Some folks were from all over the country and some were locals. Some people were quite wealthy, and others were former gang members, shot in the spinal cord.

I had private insurance, so I received the V.I.P. treatment... Or the clinic's version of it, anyway. Although none of the charges came out of my pocket, I did see statements from my insurance company on what they paid for and how much it was.

I began to wonder how some of the people attending PEERS paid for the services they received. I knew some other folks had private insurance, but I also knew some folks who took a two hour bus ride in a wheelchair for their commute to PEERS because they couldn't afford a vehicle or cab ride.

Things began not to add up. I asked over and over again when I would be using the leg braces my insurance company purchased. Since being purchased, they sat in a corner of the clinic, collecting dust. I was told over and over again I had to get strong enough to use them.

When would that be? What had to get stronger? My trunk, my chest, my arms? The day I left PEERS for good, I had yet to receive any answers to those questions.

I was a PEERS patient for almost three years. My insurance company spent over $600,000 there, and I worked very hard. I got stronger because I exercised. The brace was something Dr. Burns knew I could never functionally use and was simply a moneymaker for the program because insurance companies would purchase them.

Other things didn't make sense, either. Patients who were working side-by-side with me would suddenly stop coming to the clinic. I knew they had not completed the PEERS program because their own braces were in the same corner mine were, collecting dust. A patient of the PEERS program "graduated" when they were able to ambulate using their custom-made, orthotic RGO brace.

I received a phone call one evening after a day at PEERS. It was from a woman who brought her daughter to PEERS and had suddenly stopped coming. In a nutshell, she explained Dr. Burns kept people at PEERS until their insurance ran out.

He had absolutely no intention of getting an individual strong enough to make using the walking braces a possibility. She said he knew right off the bat 90% of his patients were not brace candidates due to the severity of their injury, and I was one of them.

The next piece of information she told me made me ill. In California, if you were shot in a gang-related incident, the state gave you $25,000 worth of health insurance if you did not have a prior felony in your background.

Dr. Burns paid an individual working at the largest rehabilitation hospital near L.A. to tell him of all the gang-related shootings in the area. Dr. Burns would then personally visit the individual in the hospital, state insurance forms in tow.

He explained to the newly injured individual he ran a ground breaking physical therapy center in Beverly Hills, specializing in people with spinal cord injuries. Dr. Burns took advantage of people in an emotionally fragile state and had them sign away the only health insurance they had over to him.

I was shocked after hearing all of this. I liked the woman who was sharing this information with me very much, and I told her I appreciated she cared enough to warn me. She said she couldn't sleep anymore without me knowing, and I was to do with the information what I wished.

A physical therapy assistant from the clinic was going to night school to get her Master's degree in physical therapy. We had become very friendly. We lived near each other and shared a love of sushi and Starbucks.

After she graduated with her Master's, she no longer worked at the clinic. We stayed in touch, but did not see as much of each other. My gut was telling me, however, she would know if this horrific information were true or not.

It was. She admitted the program's ethics were the reason she stopped working at PEERS and not because she graduated. She felt horrible not telling me, but Dr. Burns promised her if she said anything regarding how things were run at PEERS, he'd make sure her professors would know how "unfit" she was to be a physical therapist.

I said I had absolutely no hard feelings and thanked her for telling me. The next day, I went to the clinic, picked up my dusty braces and said goodbye. I told Dr. Burns my family and I felt we did not see enough improvement for me to stay three thousand miles away from home. Dr. Burns sputtered a bit, trying to convince me to stay. I lied and said my bags were already packed and I was going directly to the airport from the clinic.

A few months later, I was driving by the old brick building and I spotted big yellow tape across its doors. I found out the clinic was closed and under investigation for Medicare fraud. Whatever punishment Dr. Burns received, I guarantee he deserved more.

The Gift Of Grace

It's not always easy sharing details regarding your disability. It can, at times, leave you vulnerable to scrutiny, criticism and the worst, pity. Sharing is one thing, but I have yet to meet a disabled individual who wishes to be a poster child.

Why do it then? By telling the intimate physical, emotional, mental and social inner workings of my disability, the attention draws awareness to the extreme challenges that go along with it. The more attention a disability or disease gets, the more people will see the need for its cure.

Sharing can also be a catalyst for prevention. Much of what I share includes my personal care. The way our body works is an individual's own private information. If, however, my sharing of intimate details prevents a single person from one of the plethora of life-threatening, post-injury complications, it is well, well, worth it.

I do my best to communicate in a way that helps folks become aware whether it is physical, mental or developmental, a person's disability should not be what they are defined by. Disabled or not, we should be defined by the content of our moral character.

I have small forum to speak from. I've done inspirational speaking to groups only as large as a few hundred people, and I have my writing. You may be surprised, however, how many insulting and sarcastic comments and questions (in person and virtual) I have had thrown at me. I've even been heckled.

People act this way when they are afraid of something different they don't understand. The only way you have a chance of reaching them and getting their attention is through grace.

Grace is the act of love, kindness, mercy, favor. In other words, keep your cool and stick to the facts. Albeit, hard to do at times, but it's our only chance with ignorance on the receiving end. If you can get an individual's attention, you have an opportunity they will possibly *hear* what you are saying. That's the way you can make a difference.

Michael J. Fox has been a champion for more than twenty years in finding better treatment and a cure for Parkinson's disease. He was diagnosed with the disease in 1991 at the age of twenty-nine.

At one point in his journey with Parkinson's, he was featured on Larry King Live. He talked about his disease and promoted his latest book, "The Adventures Of An Incurable Optimist." It's an excellent read, by the way.

I found everything Michael said to be a combination of intelligent and poignant. When Larry asked Michael about Rush Limbaugh's personal attack on him, however, my jaw dropped to the floor.

It was Michael's response, or rather, the way he responded. With grace, with inspiration, with a smile. Larry wasn't giving details about the attack, so I jumped on the internet to find out more. Even now, I can't believe what I saw.

Michael J. Fox had done a televised PSA for a Democratic politician in the Midwest prior to the 2008 Presidential Election. Michael's symptoms of his disease were obvious in the PSA, as they have been many times since his diagnosis.

It is reasonable to expect someone to show the symptoms of the disease or disability they have. My wheelchair isn't an accessory. Rush Limbaugh's response to the PSA was absolutely horrific.

He actually mimicked Michael's symptoms. Limbaugh said Michael was exaggerating them for the benefit of the camera and you had never seen Michael's symptoms on television before.

When Michael responded to this attack in an extremely down to earth way. He said because many people do not understand how the symptoms and medications of Parkinson's disease work, things may look unnatural to them.

With a small but distinct window of opportunity to make a graceful response, Rush Limbaugh instead goes in the direction of a bullish bore. He had the gall to say Michael purposely skipped taking his medication prior to filming the PSA

Oh, the things I would like to say to Limbaugh. But I won't, because it will only satisfy my need of instant gratification to tell a narrow minded, ignorant conservative what I *really* think of him. I'd rather be graceful.

Okay, so I'm a work in progress.

Disability Does Not Discriminate

One of the greatest mistakes a person can make in life is the belief or perception they are invincible. The "it can't happen to me" syndrome either we or someone we know has been guilty of. It potentially leads to reckless behavior and can align circumstances in such a way that attracts catastrophe.

I recently read a story about an officer on Titanic who stated there was no fear of 'God, man or devil,' because Titanic was built so solidly it could easily withstand impact with other ships or contact with any other force; including icebergs.

Titanic was three football fields in length, twelve stories high and built of the finest materials available. A virtual fortress if ever there was one. On the fateful night of April 14, 1912, as other ships warned of icebergs ahead, Titanic steamed onward, increasing her speed through the frigid Atlantic waters.

By the time the lookouts spotted the massive iceberg in front of them, it was too late. Titanic could not turn out of harms way in time, and the rest of the story is history. Titanic, the untouchable, unsinkable, invincible ship, sank to the bottom of the ocean in less then three hours. Over 1,500 souls died.

The passengers of Titanic were of different race, class and religion. Some were commoners from different parts of Europe, heading toward America in hopes of a better life for themselves and their families. Other passengers came from some of the wealthiest families in the world.

It is said that John Jacob Astor, the richest man on the ship, had a fortune that would be worth one hundred billion dollars today. His fortune, however, made no difference in his circumstances on the night of April 14th, 1912. Despite his social standing, wealth and power, his physical wellbeing was as vulnerable as any class or race of passenger on Titanic.

If ever there was an image of an invincible human being, Christopher Reeve was it. Physically, Reeve was tall, strong and handsome. He was a wonderful family man with a loving, devoted wife who was a talented actress in her own right. He also was the father of three children.

As an actor, one of his most defining roles was of Superman, the man of steel himself. Superman could leap tall buildings in a single bound, effortlessly lift solid steel beams, capable of running faster than an express train and his skin could not be pierced.

Ladies loved him, men wanted to be him and crowds adored him. Superman *and* Reeve's, that is. Yet, despite all of his fame, affluence and accomplishments, Christopher Reeve could not escape an injury from which he would never recover.

On May 27th, 1995, Christopher Reeve sustained a spinal cord injury in an equestrian accident and almost a decade later, complications from the injury would take his life. While he was injured, he tirelessly worked to improve the life of all disabled Americans. He lobbied for stem cell research and fought to improve government benefits by trying to convince Congress it needed to widen its Medicare guidelines. I'll second that.

Professionally, he continued to work both in front of and behind the camera of Hollywood. He had access to every type of healing modality known to man, both conventional and otherwise. Yet this incredibly strong, tenacious, viral man could neither escape nor cure the shattering physical injury that befell him. You see, disabilities do not discriminate, even to Superman.

I myself am disabled from a car accident in February of 1994. It resulted in a broken neck and spinal cord injury, paralyzing me from the shoulders down. At the time, I was twenty-one years old, working as a recruiter for a Wall Street search firm and my life was a blast.

Although I had been on my own since I was seventeen, I was just beginning to feel as though my life was coming together, as I found my professional niche. I had studied English in college but had no idea what I wanted my career to be.

A Wall Street job I accepted primarily for its commi$$ion potential and benefit package ended up being something I not only did well, but more importantly, *loved* doing. It was a golden time for me.

I was making great money in a blossoming career I loved. I was meeting exciting people personally and professionally everyday. I had more than my choice of men to date. The world was my oyster. An enchanted spell settled over my life and I was under the ignorant assumption it was there to stay *just because I was me.*

That was almost twenty years ago. While my journey since has been amazing, I've eaten a few pieces of humble pie along the way. My car accident made me come to terms with the realization my twenty-one year old self was not untouchable. I was actually human.

My ego still had some learning to do. I suffered some horrific, *preventable, life-threatening* complications my doctors warned me about a thousand times since the very beginning of my injury. "Prevention is key. Prevention is key." That took a while to sink in for me.

As human beings, we all possess the same ability to experience joy, success, triumph and misfortune. Regardless of the circumstances from which you are born, you have the opportunity for luck and love, scarcity and sickness, the same as the person sitting next to you. Neither the good nor the challenges in life discriminate. They can touch us all.

Pity vs. Compassion

Language is a powerful tool, used to communicate between people. Words themselves carry immense power. The words we use, whether we are thinking to ourselves or speaking out loud, carry layers of context. A single word has the power to bring with it a whole set of underlying perceptions.

Take the word "pity" for example. Being disabled for twenty years, I have had the words said to me, "What a pity," more times than I can count as the response to my explanation of the question, "What happened to you?" When we are confronted with circumstances in life highlighting the challenges we face as human beings, particularly in responding to physical and emotional pain, we have choices on how to engage with the person experiencing the challenge. Pity is not the way to go. Compassion is.

I think pity and compassion are as different as winter and summer. The way they are spelled makes it easy to understand the difference between the two. If someone pities you, they hold you at arms length, or in a "pit." This is done to separate them from you, keeping you at a lower level then they are, as they look at you from up above.

If someone has compassion for you, the "passion" in their heart for their fellow human being makes them become involved in your circumstances. A person that pities you is similar to the doctor that gives you a pill for pain and that's it. A doctor that has compassion not only gives you pain medicine, but listens to your fears, as well.

A person who pities you says to themselves, "Well, I've done what I can do." They have met their obligation. A person that has compassion for you sees you through the challenging circumstances, that very well may be beyond their own comfort zone. They understand, however, what is more important.

People who pity you make you feel worse about your challenging circumstances than you already do. Even if someone has good intentions, how would they feel if someone said to them, "What a pity. What a shame," about their life's circumstances? I guarantee they would feel worse.

Prior to writing this article, I did a little research regarding pity and compassion… What was the true difference, especially when they are used in society so interchangeably? What made people feel good?

What made people feel bad? Did people who pity you have selfish intentions, or were they just afraid of how to react to your circumstances, therefore keeping you at arms length?

During my research, I found a healer who blogged about pity vs. compassion, and I love what she said regarding the end of her time on earth. I hope mine is the same as hers.

She said, "When I'm coming to the end of my own journey here on earth, I hope there is someone who won't just pity me and hand me a pill and say, "Call me in the morning". I've got to get through the night, and so do those around me!

No, I want a compassionate response, someone who isn't afraid of my crying, who will talk about anything or nothing, even laugh, as I make my peace and take my leave."

I can't say it any better than that.

Cap In Hand Equals Handicapped

When I was initially injured, a new life started for me. Not one I would have consciously picked, but it was mine nonetheless. My new life came with a new body, and my new body was high maintenance. It needed help with a lot of things, so I had to learn how to hire personal care aides to work with me 24/7. Of all the new things I had to get used to in my new life, this was one of the hardest… Having people around me constantly, helping me with everything you do throughout your day, beginning when you pick your head up off the pillow in the morning until you put it back down at night.

I was very naïve in the beginning. I thought every person I hired would be a modern version of Florence Nightingale…why else would you choose to work in the healthcare field? I quickly got an education of A LOT of other reasons, and some were not the best of intentions (but that's another blog in itself ☺.) One thing my family and I found frustrating was many aides sent to me from health care agencies had no idea of the care I needed, so I decided to take a personal care aide course myself to see what exactly they were taught.

Another issue I had with my new life was being called physically handicapped. It wasn't a denial thing... What was there to deny? I couldn't move from the shoulders down, so there wasn't much room for a debate there. Other similar words didn't bother me, such as physically disabled, physically challenged, individual with a disability, etc. But for some reason, handicap wanted to make me puke and punch the person using it. It still does.

At the class I took for personal care assistants, they taught almost nothing about the hands on care of another human being. They taught you how to make a bed, how to assist someone with taking medication, how to assist someone using a cane, walker or wheelchair, and not much else. They did, however, spend part of an afternoon on politically correct words and phrases and the importance of using them.

When the head instructor started talking about the origin of the word handicap, I sat up a little straighter. I learned in the early 1500's in England, homeless people who were living on the streets would often beg for money and have their cap in their hand to hold any donations they received. Over time, "cap in hand" turned into "handicap" and somehow translated into meaning a person with a disability. And we wonder how and why some words come with an instant stereotype that isn't flattering.

Every time I see a parking spot or restroom with the classic blue sign containing an outline of a person in a wheelchair, denoting the area is accommodating for someone with a disability, the word on the sign (even new signs) is handicap. Speaking politically correct, handicap has not been a popular, positive word to use when referring to a person with a disability for the last twenty years. Ironically, it's our government who needs to initiate changes for these types of signs to read something different... I guess they are having trouble catching up with themselves.

Everyone is unique in what they are sensitive to. A word or phrase that bothers one individual may not bother another, regardless of its political correctness.

Individuals with disabilities and their families have to deal with a ton of stereotypes surrounding words and phrases used to describe different physical, mental and emotional disabilities. There have been times I have used a word or phrase when referring to an individual's circumstances and they have gotten offended by my choice of words and were sure to firmly correct me.

After apologizing and reiterating I thought I was using what was correct, I always wanted to know not only what was the correct thing to say but why. This is how I realized what was correct for one person may not be correct for another.

While it's impossible to be a mind reader, before I speak to someone regarding sensitive issues, such as disabilities, I take a moment to recall my previous lessons of to say or not to say.

If you happen to say something in such a way that offends someone with a disability, the best thing to do is simply apologize sincerely and have the courage to ask them what the correct thing to say is. This will show the person you care enough to try and get it right the next time.

Think Outside The Disabled Box

A family member shared an interesting online article with me recently. A man parked in a disabled parking spot on his way to play wheelchair rugby. When he was finished and went back out to his car, there was a note waiting for him on it. The note said it was highly unlikely he was disabled, guessed his age range to be twenty-five to thirty five and (here comes my favorite part) he probably thought he "had the world by the ass." Lastly, the author offered a lame apology if he was wrong, which he made clear he did not think he was.

Let me tell you what I know from the article about the disabled man. He is paralyzed to the point of not being able to use his legs and he does not have any grip with his fingers. He is thirty-six years old, plays wheelchair rugby, works full-time, is married and drives a six year old BMW. The man who left the note probably thought he was doing a good deed, but he based his actions on assumptions, not facts.

Being disabled similarly myself, my blood boils as I watch plenty of people race into disabled parking spaces, leap out of their car as effortlessly as if they had wings and walk the few steps needed to get to their destination. To be fair, you don't have to be paralyzed and use a wheelchair full-time to need a disabled parking spot. There are dozens of legitimate reasons for a non-wheelchair user to require one. The problem is, there are thousands of people parking in them. You do the math. And I don't know if this is my imagination or not, but it always seems there are never any disabled parking spots available when it is raining or snowing or freezing cold outside, and I am forced to park somewhere in South East Asia and hike to my destination's doorway.

My brother and I experienced a similar situation as the rugby player, not long after I was first injured. We parked in a disabled parking spot at Toys R Us, which was nice and close to the entrance, just like disabled parking spots should be. I was sitting in the passenger seat, and as my brother was getting my wheelchair out of the car, I heard an elderly man start yelling.

He happened to be parked right next to us in another disabled parking spot, and had just come out of the store. He was saying something about how us young whippersnappers should be ashamed of ourselves for taking advantage of using a parking area that should be saved for someone who really needed it. His wife was not far behind him and she felt it necessary to chime in as well. My brother told the man his sister was paralyzed, but his voice fell on deaf ears as the man continued his comments.

We did what we needed to do to get me out of the car and situated. As my brother pushed me past the man's vehicle, I made eye contact with his wife. The look on her face was all I needed, and she gave her husband a stiff poke in the arm. I knew the husband saw me as well, and from that day, I have wondered if it made them think before they judged another similar situation, with no evidence except the way I looked sitting in a car seat.

What made the man write the note on the wheelchair rugby player's car? Did he think it was impossible for a disabled individual to own a BMW? And what about me? Did the elderly man find it unfathomable that a young woman could be sitting in a regular car seat and also need a wheelchair? People don't need to open their eyes, they need to open their minds.

In my experience of using a wheelchair for twenty years, I have found there is a huge social stigma surrounding individuals with disabilities. Many people are shocked that I am not bedridden, drooling, housebound or just downright utterly incompetent. It seems even more people are shocked I own my own home, am housebroken, share my home with someone whom I am in a loving relationship with, get out of bed every day, am starting my own business, enjoy travel, have friends and family I adore and spend time with or basically do anything your average human being does in a day in the life.

All of us are individuals with uniqueness distinguishing us from one another. That doesn't change if you have a disability. When I broke my neck, it paralyzed me. It did not erase everything that makes me Amy.

So the next time you feel the need to do a good deed by accusing someone of being something they aren't based solely on your assumptions, you should be prepared for the possibility you may be wrong.

A Little Courtesy, Please

Just when you think you have heard or experienced everything regarding a certain situation, life surprises you.

I am a great fan of films, and going out to see a good movie is at the top of the list of my favorite things to do. When I lived in L.A., people would fit a film in during their lunch hour, and going to a movie three or four times a week was the norm. I was in heaven.

Recently, I went to see "American Hustle." It was getting fantastic reviews and already had a lot of Oscar buzz attached to it. While My Mike went to get snacks, I sat and watched the preview trailers begin.

As I adjusted my wheelchair to get comfortable before the film started, the man sitting in front of me leaned back and barked, "Are you going to be doing that all night?!" I asked him what he meant because I honestly had absolutely no idea what he was talking about. "Is that thing going to be making noise the entire movie?" he asked with a nasty tone, nodding toward my wheelchair.

I explained the noise was my wheelchair and I couldn't help it. I was actually shocked he could hear the noise my chair made as I adjusted it over the volume of the movie previews. At most, it was a few clicks and the slightest hum that lasted a total of five or six seconds.

I told him I was moving my chair to simply get comfortable. "But am I going to have to hear that throughout the entire movie?!" Mr. Nasty asked. For a split second, I considered apologizing and saying I would try not to move at all while the movie was playing. But then I came to my senses.

"I'll have to do it occasionally. If it's going to bother you, go sit somewhere else," I said. Reasonably speaking, what human being can sit exactly in the same position for three hours and stay comfortable? Not me. I was excited to watch this film and I was going to enjoy myself.

Right before our exchange began, My Mike had come back. He was seated to my right, next to the wall. The gentleman with the questions was sitting directly in front of me, and his wife was sitting to his right. The door to the theater was directly to my left. I had already decided if the man chose to stand up and continue his ridiculousness, I would simply leave the theater. I knew My Mike would be right behind me without a word. I would get the manager to address this jerk...I was not going to miss the film or get into a pissing contest with Mr. Nasty.

Luckily, Mr. Nasty decided to stay in his seat and the exchange between us ended there. The film was great and I watched it comfortably, as I adjusted my chair when I needed to. The man in front of me either didn't hear the noise my chair made or figured it wasn't worth to mention it. His wife sat as still as a statue for the entire film and neither of them looked our way as they left.

In twenty years of using a wheelchair, this encounter was the first of its kind for me. I have been hit by a car in my wheelchair, while crossing a boulevard by a jerk driver in a hurry. I have had everything from clothing to cash to credit cards to my vehicle stolen from me by personal care aides who worked for me.

I have gone to the movies many times and had to ask the able-bodied person sitting in the companion seat in the disabled section of the theater to please move and their nose has gotten extremely bent out of joint. But complaining about the noise my wheelchair makes as I move it was a first. Has our society gotten so wrapped up with ourselves we have become this intolerant? I feel I need to wear a sign saying, "A little courtesy, please."

Before I was injured, I was at the movie theater and a disabled girl was sitting behind me with a few of her friends. Her disability must have been quite severe because she had a large power wheelchair and used a ventilator. Throughout the film, I could hear the whoosh as the ventilator breathed in and out for her, and every ten or fifteen minutes I heard a small series of beeps.

My friends and I did not say a word. Nor did we have any desire to. Nor did we sit in our seats, wishing we were sitting somewhere else. It was a little bit of noise coming from a human being I am sure would rather be in different circumstances. If we thought anything, it was bravo to her for going out with her girlfriends to enjoy a good film, just like any body else... The key word being "body"... Able body, disabled body, ANY BODY.

I pray with my whole heart the lack of intolerance I experienced from the man in the theater is not where society is headed. I am very aware there are and probably always will be a percentage of the population living in this frame of mind. I consider myself an optimist, yet it seems to me I am experiencing more and more of these types of encounters than I used to.

I hope I am wrong. But if I'm not, I hope there is a shift in society, embracing patience and understanding towards people who may be different than our majority. Every BODY deserves to be accommodated.

Discrimination...I No Longer Care

For the first two decades of my life, I never experienced discrimination. I knew what discrimination was, of course, but I knew it from a distance. Like a cousin once removed.

All that changed after I broke my neck and became paralyzed when I was twenty-one. Being disabled, I was treated entirely differently than before I became disabled, not only by strangers, but even some people I knew. People spoke to me as if I were deaf, would not look me in the eye or stared at me with a look of disgust, pity or "stay away, you're contagious."

Complete strangers asked me the rudest, most personal questions that were absolutely none of their business. People treated me as if I had the IQ of a slug and at times, like the elephant in the room that nobody talks about or talks to. Discrimination at its finest.

This struck me as so odd because it took about ten seconds to become disabled...That's how long it takes to become paralyzed once your neck cracks and your spinal cord is injured... Had I really changed so much in that amount of time?

Twenty years later, none of this has changed. Discrimination still meets and greets me almost every day. The difference is, I no longer care. Being treated with discrimination no longer brings me to tears, leaving me wondering what I had done wrong and how I could change it.

If people were going to show discrimination towards me because I had a disability, there was nothing I could do to change the way they thought. I could, however, control my perception of how I see myself instead of turning that power over to ignorant individuals.

I was going to come in contact with people who discriminate towards me for the rest of my life because my injury is permanent. Like race, ethnic background and sexuality... three heavy hitters in the discrimi-nation department...I can't change my disability anymore than I can change the color of my skin.

Realizing my perception needed changing did not happen overnight. It was a process I was almost unaware of, until at one point in time I couldn't remember the last time experiencing discrimination hurt my feelings. To be clear, not the last time I experienced discrimination, but the last time it cut like a knife.

As most personal growth goes, it's much easier said than done. I've had twenty years of practice dealing with discrimination; other people have experienced it their entire lives. And while practice does not make perfect, it can come pretty damn close. Don't give your personal power away to people who judge a book by its cover instead of its contents.

Chapter 5:
KIDS ARE MY GREATEST INSPIRATION

Pissy Missy

I am truly blessed in life with the wonderful group of individuals surrounding me. I feel, however, there is one individual in particular that needs to be recognized.

My cat, Missy. She is one of my kids. My oldest nephew dubbed her "Pissy Missy" when he was nine or ten years old. It fits her perfectly. Most cats possess a certain amount of attitude. When the Universe made Missy, she was given an extra helping.

Missy rules our house. We have a pony, a horse, (our other two kids), personal care aides and two grown adults sharing a home along with Missy. She has everyone manipulated and tripping over themselves to get her what she desires.

Part of the problem is she is very beautiful. Stunning. I know all parents say their child is the prettiest, but with Missy, it's true. She is a long-haired calico, with the most perfect color combination and markings I have ever seen.

She has bright green eyes. At times, depending on their slant, they make her look like she has a bit of the devil in her. Literally.

I adopted Missy when I lived in L.A. I had put the word out through my friends I wanted to adopt a cat. I worked at a Humane Society when I was in college and it was very important to me to adopt an animal needing a home. I was hoping to be the interception between someone not being able to keep their cat and the Humane Society.

Along came Missy. She wasn't quite a year old and her owner was moving back to Sweden and could not take her. Missy had been abused as a kitten and her current owner had saved her. Missy suffered from PTSD and was very jumpy. We were a perfect match. I deal with PTSD from being in a car accident and can be quite jumpy myself.

Missy's owner brought her over to meet me about a week before she moved. She explained how she had acquired Missy, what Missy liked to eat and that Missy liked to be talk to in a soft voice. My lungs were partially paralyzed from my injury and my voice was naturally low. It seemed Missy and I were destined for each other.

When Missy moved in, I didn't see her for three days. I kept food, water and her litter box outside on my balcony. I had a kitty door installed so she could access her things whenever she liked.

For those first three days, Missy hid in my apartment loft. Each night, after my aide left and all was quiet, I could hear her chewing on the cat food and lapping up water.

Finally, she felt safe enough to make her presence known. It was early in the morning and I was waiting for my aide to come to work. Missy jumped on my bed and settled herself on my chest, with her chin right underneath mine.

I was thrilled. I spoke to her softly and thanked her for coming out in the daylight. I lived on the third floor of an apartment building. Every time a car went by or there was a noise on the street, Missy crouched down and the pupils of her eyes got really big. She would stay on my chest and try to make herself as flat as a pancake.

As time went on, Missy grew braver. She'd venture out onto the balcony to lay on the top rail, tails swishing, pupils dilated, watching the action on the street below.

At times, Missy was my only companion. I was three thousand miles away from home. When an aide pulled a no call, no show, it was Missy who was my company. I kept my phone in bed with me at night in case I had an aide issue in the morning, but this plan was not foolproof.

Sometimes I would move my arms too much at night and was unable to reach the phone in the morning when it was clear my aide had no intention of coming to work. I'd have to lay in bed, and wait for my next shift to show up at 3 p.m.

If I was frustrated or scared, Missy would lick my tears away with her little sand paper tongue. She never left my side. Even while I was getting ready for my day... Missy would lay on the opposite side of the bed as a watchman.

I moved from L.A. to New York about thirteen years ago. Prior to my move, I sold everything in my apartment except my pictures, my plants, my shoes and my cat. Missy was a world traveler. From Sweden, to L.A. to N.Y., her and her attitude fit right in.

I think most people would say their pets are their family. These are creatures who love us unconditionally and are always happy to see us. How many creatures can you say that about?

How Many Tokens Are You?

For Christmas this year, my nine year old nephew asked if he and I could go out together for the afternoon. He wanted to start with Toys "R" Us and then onto Chucky Cheese...Every kid's dream and every parent's headache. But if you're an aunt, it's a blast!

Toys"R" Us was fun. My nephew, Zac, had gift cards from Christmas to spend, and he was determined to buy Lego sets. I had strict instructions from Zac's mom he could buy anything *except* Legos. He has boxes and boxes of them at home, some still unopened.

I had no idea how many toys Lego made. Zac tried his hardest to convince me he desperately needed a multitude of Star War Lego kits. I think we went down four aisles before we saw a brand other than Lego.

He settled on two gigantic Nerf guns, and helped me pick out a belated Christmas gift for his younger brother. Toys "R" Us is a dangerous store... Even for adults. I was proud of Zac. Once his gift card amount was spent, he was happy to leave without an ounce of "But I really need *this,* too."

Chucky Cheese was total chaos when we arrived. It was Sunday, and I realized I had never been there on a weekend. Dozens upon dozens of kids were playing all sorts of games. Some little ones were screaming because their parents said it was time to go home. By Chucky's stage, a few birthday parties were simultaneously celebrating.

I was trying my best not to step on little feet. We found a table, ordered some pizza and bought tokens for the games. Zac went to play a basketball type game, and I followed a few steps behind.

As I kept an eye on Zac, I wandered around nearby, checking out the games other kids were playing. It was fun to see four year olds in competition with each other, with the victor getting so excited!

Suddenly, this tiny little dark haired girl comes out of nowhere and climbs on my lap as quick as a mini gecko. She kicks her shoes off, settles herself on her knees and is instantly comfortable on my lap.

She realizes she's forgotten something and turns around to look at me. She was perhaps three years old and no bigger than a peanut. She had a blue dress on, colorful tights and the longest, darkest eyelashes I had ever seen.

She fearlessly looks me in the eye, smiles and asked," How many tokens are you?" She was so quick, so unafraid and so damn cute, all I could do was smile. She thought I was a ride.

Less then a minute went by from the time she climbed on my lap to when she asked how many tokens I required. Chucky Cheese was very crowded. This girl was too little to be left playing on her own. My eyes began to scan the crowd for someone who looked like they may be looking for their child.

Suddenly, my eyes locked with a woman on the far side of the restaurant. The look on her face said everything. She set off towards us as fast as she could. I wanted to start weaving my way through the crowd to meet her, but I worried she would lose sight of us and panic.

So I stayed where I was, with her daughter on my lap. I waved to the woman and she waved back frantically. I smiled and hoped she could tell I was going to stay where I was until she got to us. I felt so bad because she had to watch her little girl sit on a complete stranger's lap.

It was slow going for her to get to us. There was literally no room to move through people. By this time, the little peanut told me her name was Sara and asked why we weren't moving. She showed me her cup of tokens and asked me again how many I needed.

I didn't bother explaining. I just told her my name and said we were going to wait until her mom came to us. She pointed to the birthday party she was a part of and said she was big enough to play the games with seats.

At that moment, her mom reached us. She grabbed Sara, and went back and forth with thank you and apologies. I introduced myself, and told her no apology necessary because I adore children. The woman's name was Naomi. She said out of her four children, Sara was the youngest and by far, the fastest.

My table was next to her birthday party, so we walked back together. Sara wanted to ride on my lap, and I said I wouldn't mind in the least. I think Naomi, however, needed to carry her daughter because Sara was persistent about the lap ride and Naomi said nothing.

Imagine being at a crowded place like Chucky Cheese and seeing your daughter on a stranger's lap *on the other side of the room*. The poor woman must have been terrified of the possibilities of my intentions.

Naomi and Sara went back to their birthday party. Normally, I explain to little kids I have a big boo-boo and it makes my legs not work. They usually think the wheelchair is cool and love the joystick.

That day, however, I didn't explain anything to Sara. I preferred to stay as a ride at Chucky Cheese.

You Can Do It, Dad! Just Spank'erass.

This story has absolutely nothing to do with being disabled. It is just too funny not to share.

I was at my friend Andrea's house for dinner. It was just some family, about eight of us.

Andrea and her husband, Ross, have three beautiful children. At the time, the oldest, Zac, was five, Julia took the middle spot at three, and Cameron was almost one.

We were having dinner in the dining room, enjoying wonderful food and good red wine. All of a sudden, we hear a blood curdling, hair-raising scream from Cameron. The kind of scream that said he was hurt.

Poor Andrea couldn't get to him fast enough. All three kids were in the living room. Zac was watching television, Cameron was in his walker seat and Miss Julia was up to mischief.

If you saw Julia with Cameron now, she is his biggest protector. When he was first born, however, she had the jealousy that naturally comes along with no longer being the baby.

Cameron was screaming in his chair. Julia was standing right next to him. As Andrea picked up her screaming baby, her mother's instinct told her Julia was the cause.

After making sure Cameron was okay and handing him to a relative, Andrea demanded Julia tell her what she did. After being "asked" by her mother a second time, Julia confessed to biting Cameron on the arm.

Julia got a spanking and was sent to her room screaming. She not only slammed the door of her bedroom upstairs, but she continued to open and slam the door while screaming the entire time.

Ross had not made a move. Andrea wanted him to go upstairs and spank Julia again. Without looking up from his plate, Ross simply said, "I don't want to."

The rest of us were looking at our own plates, in an attempt to not crack up with laughter. Andrea started yelling at her husband. She insisted they were going to be failures as parents if they didn't follow through with discipline.

Ross sighed and pushed his chair away from the table to get up and go deal with his daughter. Suddenly, from the peanut gallery in the living room, you hear a little boy's voice say with encouragement and enthusiasm, "You can do it, Dad! Just spank her ass!"

That was all it took. We all started crying with laughter, including Andrea and Ross. Zac repeated his support. Ross thanked his son and said he was on his way.

Zac had obviously learned that phrase from his parents, which was funny enough. But what really had us rolling was the way he said it. It came out as one word..."Spank'erass." He was only five. He probably truly thought it was one word.

I am cracking up as I write this. It's one of those stories you laugh about every time it crosses your mind. "Just spank'erass." It should be on a T-shirt or bumper sticker.

Zac is nine now. He and Julia remember that night and all three kids love to hear the story. Once when I was telling the three of them the story for the millionth time, Cameron asked his sister, "Sissy, why did you *bite* me?" Julia wordlessly looked at him, picked up his arm, and kissed the spot she had bitten. Cameron smiled.

A Voice Of Our Future

On September 30th, 2008, my foundation held its tenth annual golf outing. The Amy Alexander Foundation for Spinal Cord Injuries provides financial aide to myself and other people like me, living with spinal cord injuries.

When I was first injured, my math teacher from eighth grade visited me at home and presented me with a wonderful gift; a non-profit foundation in my name. It was a vehicle I could grow with and the money in it would not affect my eligibility for any financial aide I received from the government.

Our first fund- raiser twenty years ago was a penny social. We raised about $1,200.00. Now, our annual golf outing is sold out each year and we have raised as much as $25,000.00 – $30,000.00 in a single outing. 2008's outing was going to be our tenth, and we wanted to make it extra spectacular for our golfers and another significant financial success.

I am always so proud to have my name on such a first class event. We always had a hole in one, with a brand-new vehicle as the prize. For our landmark tenth outing, we had two beautiful brand new Jeeps for a hole-in-one winner. We also had gorgeous beer cart girls attending to our thirsty golfers throughout the day, a few margarita bars set up on the course, a photographer so golfers could purchase pictures at the end of the day, cigars, a fantastic dinner and other fun filled amenities.

I felt the best feature of the day was my nine year old niece. Every year at our outing, before the shotgun start at 11:00 a.m., we have a local talent sing the Star Spangled Banner. About a month prior to the outing, my niece Jamie asked if she could be the person to sing it for our tenth anniversary.

After auditioning for our board, consisting of five family members and friends, we unanimously agreed she would be our singer. Jamie and I spent a lot of time together on a regular basis and I had listened to her sing a thousand times, including the Star Spangled Banner. She had a beautiful, clear voice and it meant so much to me she would be our event opener.

Nonetheless, I, nor anyone else, was prepared for the performance she gave. My niece, microphone in hand, with the sun shining on her golden head, turning her into a mini modern angel, belted out the Star Spangled Banner like a pro. She was amazing...her voice was clear, sweet and strong, her pitch was perfect, and she hit the high notes as if they were nothing.

As she hung on the last note, the crowd burst into applause. It was impossible not to. When she put the microphone down and ran over to me to throw her arms around my neck, I couldn't stop smiling. As the applause stopped, I leaned back to look at the beaming face of the little girl standing before me, and in that moment, a wave of tremendous pride, excitement and hope washed over me.

Jamie embodied everything we, as individuals and as a country, were striving for and needing to be...confident in their abilities, courageous about their fears, excited and enthusiastic about the possibilities of what new experiences could bring, open-minded regarding change, and kind, supportive and giving to their fellow man.

With everything challenging in our world today, I find myself wondering sometimes what will our future be? Who will lead us? I looked into the shining eyes of this little girl in front of me, full of passion for life and optimism. As I realized all throughout our world there were thousands of young people with the same look in their eyes, I suddenly knew what our future would be and who would be leading us.

Disney On Disability

It's simply impossible not to love the way a child's mind works. If you are in a challenging situation and need to find the silver lining, just ask a kid. What they see is so honest because they have no hidden agenda.

I went to Disney World for the first time when I was thirty-three years old. In my opinion, even for an adult, Disney World is an extraordinary place to visit. There are dozens of things to do for every spirit. Whether you are adventurous and enjoy the fast rides and steep roller coasters, or would rather spend time in the milder exhibits, Disney has something for every one of every age.

It was a family vacation. The nephew and niece I went with were eleven and seven at the time, and we had a blast together. On the flight there, I promised I would figure out a way to go on every single ride with them. I kept a roll of duct tape in my knapsack in case we needed it to keep me from falling out of a ride. I have used duct tape many times... ultra-lighting, skydiving and SCUBA.

I needn't have worried. My brother and brother-in-law were my muscle to get on and off each ride. For the rides that were fast, steep and went upside down, I was sandwiched between the two of them, with our arms linked together. I had no fear of falling out because they had such a grip on me. I think I was safer than the folks with only the seatbelts to hold them in.

The people who worked at Disney were amazing. Even if my family were unable to help me, I would have been fine. In fact, the Disney folks running the rides looked embarrassed and apologized many times when there was really nothing for them to do in assisting us.

We had our system down pat by the second ride. My brother-in-law would get on the ride, my brother would pick me up and hand me to him, my brother-in-law would hold me until my brother got on the ride as well, and then they both got me safe and settled. Our system took about ten seconds.

My nephew and niece were thrilled about two things. First, people in wheelchairs and the people accompanying them did not have to wait in any lines. Second, we were allowed to stay on a ride multiple times without having to get off. Now, to an eleven and seven year old, this was heaven. Shear heaven.

Their smiles took up their entire faces as we breezed past dozens of exhausted people waiting in two hours worth of winding lines. At one point, after staying on the coveted "River Raft" ride at least four times, a little boy standing in line with whom I assume were his exasperated parents gave my niece a longing look as she got off our raft, soaking wet and laughing. She gave him a haughty look, shook her hair at him and said, "Don'tcha wish your aunt was in a wheelchair?!"

Self-pity is an extremely addictive, dangerous emotion that's always right around the corner. It waits to indulge you at a weak moment, promising to give you the high you need. Like your very own personal heroin dealer.

I had an amazing time on our Disney World family vacation. My nephew and niece were at a great age to go, and I kept my promise, going on every ride with them. Multiple times. It was no hardship for me... I could ride roller coasters every day. I love feeling your stomach is in your throat.

My experience could have been much different. I could have been sad, watching thousands of able bodied aunts and uncles and parents go on rides with their children and not needing any special accommodations. Obviously it crossed my mind or I wouldn't be mentioning it.

But why give in to the emotional heroin? You hate yourself afterwards, and the more times you give in, the harder it is to say no the next time it presents itself. Besides, what's the big deal of needing a wheelchair when it means you don't have to wait on lines at Disney World?

My Greatest Inspiration

The greatest inspiration in my life is, without a doubt, the children in it. I have seven nieces and nephews, the oldest being thirty-two and the youngest being four. I do not distinguish which ones are on my boyfriend's side of our family and which ones are on mine... I fell in love with each of them at first sight and love them all equally.

I'm crazy about kids. I have been as long as I can remember. I think it stemmed from being the youngest of my siblings, with my brother and sister being eight and eleven years older than me. I always wanted a younger brother or sister to play with, teach things to and be able to observe their amazing growth process. Like watching a flower grow from a seed into a beautiful blossom.

When I was about thirteen years old, I got my wish. I didn't get a younger brother or sister, but if did get my first babysitting job. I became a regular babysitter for two sweetie pie kids, a little boy and a little girl. The boy was about three and the little girl was still crawling. I was in heaven.

The more time I spent with them, the easier it was for me to see why I craved children so much. Children are everything you want in an ideal human being. They say what they mean, they mean what they say, they call a spade a spade, they have no hidden agenda, they wear their hearts on their sleeve and they just want to have fun! Try finding all of those inspiring qualities in people we know, including ourselves. Plenty of room for improvement in me when I compare myself with a kid.

Webster's defines inspiration as "…someone or something that causes the state of being stimulated to special or unusual activity, or an idea or action resulting from this state." For me, simply put, inspiration is what lights me up. What thought or image instantly brings on the feeling of passion and excitement about life?

When we start a new journey in life, inspiration is invaluable. A must. Every day you will take baby steps as a pioneer, slowly and steadily creating the new adventure you have chosen for yourself. Inevitably, doubt will creep its way in, at times the size of raindrops and other times a flood. At these times, immerse yourself in inspiration.

Living with a spinal cord injury is a journey requiring heavy doses of inspiration. There are times when I am filled with doubt and confusion, and I need inspiration like I need air. In the beginning of living with a spinal cord injury, I thought if I experienced any doubt or fear, it would simply take over and I would forever be a coward. I had to learn courage was not the absence of doubt or fear but instead, courage is continuing on your journey without letting the doubt or fear stop you.

If you hit doubt hard enough, with enough high-powered inspiration, it will slowly slink away. If you have the courage to stand up to doubt with inspiration, you'll notice as you continue on your new journey, doubt will come back less and less. Until one day, you won't be able to remember the last time you felt it.

CONCLUSION

I believe to inspire someone, you must get their attention. To do this, you must touch their heart. Nothing does this better than the truth.

My greatest wish for you, the reader, is to find my stories relatable to your stories. Everyone has their wheelchairs. More importantly, every one can get past them and move onward and upward.

This book is just scratching the surface of the vision for, "What's Your Wheelchair?" Self growth and self improvement are not something we should practice only in times of crisis. It's something we should make a part of our daily routine. Like brushing our teeth.

As we consciously make self growth and self improvement a part of our day, it will subconsciously become a part of who we are. We will no longer have to think about it. It will simply become our lifestyle.

With any process, we need tools. As it evolves, "What's Your Wheelchair?" will provide the tools necessary for a lifestyle of continued self growth and self improvement. Tools that work and tools that are *fun.*

Currently on our website, www.WhatsYourWheelchair.com, I post new articles weekly and you can archive previously posted ones.

You can also sign up to be notified via email as new articles are posted and easily share us with social media.

In the extreme near future, our website will offer products and services currently available in the self help arena. All items available have our highest recommendation, as we would not offer something we have not used ourselves with successful results.

When you have an injury like mine, currently incurable by the conventional and unconventional medical community, you are presented by dozens of people with hundreds of "sure things."

Sure cures for my injury and guaranteed ways of making millions of dollars overnight are always the heavy hitters. But I've been approached for cures, guarantees and sure things regarding every life issue imaginable. "Sure things" are sure to do one thing - disappoint.

An exciting self improvement organization has introduced itself on our horizon. Quanta International, LLC., is founded by two extremely well respected entrepreneurs, Jim Britt and Jim Lutes.

I believe an individual's intentions play a major role with the success of their company. Quanta International's founders, both already extremely successful businessmen, created a company with a vision to truly enrich people's lives personally and financially while benefiting its Affiliates.

When you visit our website at www.WhatsYourWheelchair.com/self-improvement, you'll learn more about the company's founders, their programs and the opportunities of becoming involved. "What's Your Wheelchair, Inc." is a proud Affiliate, along with thousands of other Affiliates in the self improvement circle.

I hope you liked my book. Visit WhatsYourWheelchair.com for a continue of new stories and to stay updated on the latest additions to our project!

My very best wishes to you, and thanks for reading.

Amy

www.ingramcontent.com/pod-product-compliance
Lightning Source LLC
Chambersburg PA
CBHW071004040426
42443CB00007B/660